War Crimes, Atrocity, and Justice

War Crimes, Atrocity, and Justice

Michael J. Shapiro

polity

The right of Michael J. Shapiro to be identified as Author of this Work has been asserted in accordance with the UK Copyright, Designs and Patents Act 1988.

First published in 2015 by Polity Press

Polity Press
65 Bridge Street
Cambridge CB2 1UR, UK

Polity Press
350 Main Street
Malden, MA 02148, USA

ISBN-13: 978-0-7456-7154-3 (hardback)
ISBN-13: 978-0-7456-7155-0 (paperback)

A catalogue record for this book is available from the British Library.

Typeset in 11 on 13 pt Sabon
by Toppan Best-set Premedia Limited
Printed and bound in Great Britain by TJ International Ltd, Padstow, Cornwall

The publisher has used its best endeavors to ensure that the URLs for external websites referred to in this book are correct and active at the time of going to press. However, the publisher has no responsibility for the websites and can make no guarantee that a site will remain live or that the content is or will remain appropriate.

Every effort has been made to trace all copyright holders but if any have been inadvertently overlooked the publisher will be pleased to include any necessary credits in any subsequent reprint or edition.

For further information on Polity, visit our website:
politybooks.com

Contents

Preface and Acknowledgments

Early on in his history of pornography, *The Secret Museum*, Walter Kendrick remarks that historically pornography has not been a thing; it has been an argument. The same can be said of war crimes. I have become sensitive to the homology between Kendrick's and my subject matter thanks to productive discussions with my editors, Louise Knight and Pascal Porcheron at Polity, about what to put on the cover, and to my conversations with Dr Keanu Sai, a Hawaiian scholar, who with other members of Hawaii's shadow government (officials of "The Hawaiian Kingdom," a formerly recognized state that was illegally overthrown in 1893 by a militia of US citizens, spurred by sugar planters and descendants of missionaries), secured legal counsel to lodge a war crimes complaint at the International Criminal Court at The Hague.

War crimes are not unambiguous objects of representation. To borrow a phrase from Jacques Rancière, a war crime is a phenomenon that "leaves representation in ruins by shattering any harmonious relationship between presence and absence, between the material and the intelligible." In accord with that disharmony, my investigation relies on non-representational philosophical discourses for conceptual framing and on the arts for illustrations that resist closure. With respect to the latter, I am deeply indebted to two novels, my engagement with which provides the bookends of my text: Mathias Énard's *Zone*, whose main protagonist is headed to Rome to place a trove of material on atrocities that have occurred in the Mediterranean area in the Vatican archives, and Laszlo Krasznahorkai's *War and War*, whose protagonist heads to New York (which he regards as the "new Rome,") to place a manuscript on war on the Internet.

Other debts have been incurred as I worked on and presented some of the chapters at various academic venues. The names of people whose help and/or inspiration I wish to acknowledge include those to whom I am indebted for the individual lecture and conference invitations that prompted the prototypes of chapters, to those who inspired me by reading and responding to drafts, to those who inspired me in general by example (some of whom I served with on panels at professional meetings), to those who encouraged me in discussions about my ideas for the book, and to students who helped me formulate my approach to my analyses as I discussed them in my courses. The list, in alphabetical order, without role differentiation includes: Anna Agathangelou, Elena dell'Agnese, Linda Åhäll, Rune Saugman Anderson, Florentina Andreescu, Jens Bartelson, Paul Battersby, Jane Bennett, Bettina Brown, Cesare Casarino, Charmain Chuae, Bill Connolly, Elizabeth Dauphinee, James Der Derian, Mick Dillon, Jenny Edkins, Brad Evans, Thomas Gregory, Jairus Grove, Julia Peres Guimarães, Marjaana Jauhola, Andy Kear, Garnet Kindervater, Chuck Lawrence, Luis Lobo Guerrero, Tom Lundborg, John Mowitt, Peter Narby, Michelle Pace, Sami Pihlström, François-Xavier Plasse-Couture, Sam Opondo, Julian Reid, Nick Robinson, Mark Salter, Peer Schouten, Manfred Steger, Hannah Tavares, Corey Walker-Mortimer, Andreja Zevnik.

Shorter prototypes of three of the chapters in this book have been previously published: "Life's Contested

Dispositifs: Apparatuses of Capture/Exuberant Lines of Flight," *Theory & Event* 16: 4 (2013); "Justice and the Archives: 'The Method of Dramatization'," in Jenny Edkins and Adrian Kear, eds. *International Politics and Performance: Critical Aesthetics and Creative Practice* (Routledge, 2014); and "War Crimes: The Justice *Dispositif*," in Paul Battersby, Joseph Siracusa, and Manfred Steger, eds. *The SAGE Handbook of Globalization* (Sage, 2014). I am grateful to the publishers for granting permission for republication.

Introduction

My inquiry into war crimes, atrocities, and justice in this book mobilizes political and philosophical concepts and deploys them on global spaces, forces, and events, primarily (but not exclusively) as they are articulated through artistic texts. I focus on such texts because aesthetically oriented approaches to life-worlds provoke critical thinking. They "destabilize the epistemic ground;"[1] their "heteroglossia"[2] (clash of centrifugal voices, in the case of literature, and montage of images, in the case of cinema) challenge the unreflective protocols of official and institutionalized sense making; and crucially for my investigations, they evince a "literary justice," which in contrast to "legal justice," keeps issues open and available for continuous reflection rather than imposing definitive judgments.[3]

As is well known, "literature is not verifiable,"[4] as Gayatri Spivak has put it; it will not offer definitive judgments about what should be known. In the face of such epistemic uncertainty, what can an inquiry into war crimes and justice, which foregrounds reflections in literature and film on the interrelationships between epistemological, ethical, and political fields, offer that social science investigations cannot? Spivak's suggestion is that "the protocols of fiction give us a practical simulacrum of the graver discontinuities inhabiting (and operating?) the ethico-epistemic and ethico-political...an experience of the discontinuities that remain in place in 'real life'." Fiction, as an "event – an indeterminate 'sharing' between the writer and reader" can provide an "angle of vision" that provokes thinking rather than offering definitive knowledge judgments.[5]

The angles of vision operating in fictional texts are effectively invitations to the reader to consider the indeterminacy of positions that afflict all ethico-epistemic and ethico-political perspectives. What I take from such affliction is an imperative to reflect on and add complexity to rather than seek definitive judgments about such contentious and undeconstructable concepts as war crimes and justice. And crucially, rather than seeing writers/investigators and readers as fixed subjects who stand in a stable epistemological field, I suggest that we regard them as historically evolving personae, as becoming subjects who are, in M. M. Bakhtin's terms, "unconsummated"; they are subjects who are... "axiologically yet to be."[6]

Accordingly, the style of my writing, articulated as a series of interventions, must reflect my aim to resist certainties and provoke thinking rather than offering definitive explanations. Each chapter is an essay rather than an attempt at explanatory closure. The significance of the essay form for political inquiry is its experimental mode. As John O'Neill has put it:

> It is an experiment in the community of truth, and not a packaging of knowledge ruled by definitions and operations. The essay is a political instrument inasmuch as it liberates the writer and reader from the domination of conventional standards of clarity and communication... [it's a] basic expression of literary initiative... accomplished against the limits of received language.[7]

Stylistically, my text throughout this book therefore contains minimal explication and unmediated information reporting, and instead functions largely through juxtaposition, through what Walter Benjamin, referring to *his* style, called "literary montage." With that mode of writing one *shows* connections among parallel forces and events rather than elaborately explaining how they interrelate.[8] Nevertheless, my objects of analysis are drawn from the historical realities that provoke questions about war crimes, atrocities, and justice. Although much of what I am calling my style is influenced by the aesthetic orientations of the arts – especially literature and cinema – I'd like to assume that the writing style through which my investigation proceeds amounts to "a stylistic drop in an ocean of reality."[9]

Because much of my analysis throughout this investigation is inspired by my encounters with literary texts, part of what I hope to show is how literature's imaginative constructions of space and time disrupt entrenched and unreflective ways of seeing/interpreting life-worlds; "[l]iterature selects, develops and confronts signs in different worlds, along different aspects of time according to differing processes of continuous variation or transversals [this is what] [Gilles] Deleuze calls a writer's 'style'."[10]

To illustrate the value of such a style as it applies to my objects of analysis, I turn to a brief reflection on an extraordinarily profound and politically perspicuous story by Zadie Smith, "The Embassy of Cambodia," which in an oblique yet critically focused way is about war crimes and atrocities.[11] The story's protagonist is an African household servant, Fatou, a displaced Ivorian from Accra, Ghana, a city that exports servants and welcomes tourists.[12] Fatou works as a maid for the Derawals, a mini-mart franchise-owning, Anglo-Indian family, residing in the North London suburb of Willesden. In the story, London's Cambodian Embassy is unobtrusively located in Fatou's suburban neighborhood. The embassy's less-than-grand edifice ("It is only a four- or five-bedroom, North London suburban villa") is "surrounded by a red brick wall about eight feet high,"[13] which Fatou often passes on her way to swim at a private club.

Two kinds of access are contrasted in Fatou's journey from the Derawal household to the pool, which provides her with moments of pleasurable escape from her confined life. Although it is the Derawals and not Fatou who are members of the club, Fatou has access to the pool because while the Derawals are absent from the house on Mondays she draws from "a stock pile of guest passes" in the drawer of a hallway console where "Nobody besides Fatou seems to remember that they are there."[14] As one with no ownership resources except her own canny observational skills, Fatou uses "tactics" rather than "strategies"; she makes use of temporality, the seizing of moments, rather than the strategies available to those who control space.[15] Fatou's access to the embassy is limited to what she can see and hear from the outside. As she passes it, she becomes aware of a badminton game continually underway behind the wall. She sees a shuttlecock arcing "back and forth, cresting this wall horizontally," and hears the hits, "Pock, smash. Pock, smash."[16] What is the significance of those onomatopoeias: "pock, smash?"

As the story progresses, the reader is introduced to Fatou's speculations about atrocity in two different venues. First, she thinks about the violence perpetrated on household servants: "In a discarded *Metro* found on the floor of the Derawal kitchen," she reads "a story about a Sudanese 'slave' living in a rich man's house in London" and ponders: "It was not the first time that Fatou had wondered if she herself was a slave." Then she wonders about the violence associated with various mass killings. For example, thinking about the Cambodian extermination campaign, she says to her Nigerian friend Andrew Okonkwo (employed as a night guard) that "more people died in Rwanda…And nobody speaks about that! Nobody!"[17] Shouldn't we therefore be associating those "pock smashes" with the torture deaths carried out by the Khmer Rouge? Brilliantly, Smith's story displays a "transversal eye;"[18] it provides for "new visions" as it effects a transversality between the atrocities carried out by national regimes, which draw insufficient attention, and the even more hidden atrocities experienced by migrant domestic servants. Unlike ethnographic subjects, who through visits to the sites of the Cambodian atrocities and interviews with witnesses and victims, convey a deepened sense of the experience of the atrocities, Fatou is an "aesthetic subject"[19] through whom the text thinks as it reframes the atrocity phenomenon. Because she is constituted as a liminar, who experiences a different kind of atrocity, her story serves to broaden the atrocity problematic rather than intensify the experiences associated with a particular historical moment.

With respect to the lack of visibility of national level atrocities, much is made in the story of how surprising it is that the Cambodian Embassy of London is located out of the center. As the story's narrator puts it, "we [the residents of Willesden] were surprised by the appearance of the Cambodian Embassy...It is not the right sort of surprise somehow."[20] And in addition to the mention of Rwandan atrocities, about which "nobody speaks" (Fatou's remark to her Nigerian friend, Andrew), Andrew brings up the Hiroshima atomic bombing in which, as he puts it, "They killed five million people in *one second*." The narrative goes on to have Fatou realize "that she had heard the story before...But she felt the same vague impatience with it as she did with all accounts of suffering in the distant past, for what could be done about the suffering of the past?" Fatou's impatience with thinking about past atrocities is given a more general resonance earlier in the story, when the narrator representing the "people of Willesden" notes that they have "some sympathy" for the kind of fascination with the Cambodian Embassy's "strangely compelling aura,"[21] but adds, "The fact is if we followed the history of every little country in this world...we would have no space left in which to live our own lives or to apply ourselves to necessary tasks..."[22]

Thus the story implies that the hiddenness of war crimes and atrocities is owed as much to the psychic suppressions of the phenomenology of everyday life as it is to suppression strategies of government-controlled media.

With respect to the domestic venues of atrocity, it is evident that the Derawal household has been a cruel, carceral space for Fatou. Although she has not been brutally beaten, "Mrs Derawal had twice slapped her in the face, and the two older children spoke to her with no respect at all and thanked her for nothing. (Sometimes she heard her name used as a term of abuse between them: 'You're as black as Fatou.' Or 'You're as stupid as Fatou.')". And she is trapped. The Derawals' household serves as a relay for the global management of "traceablility"[23] and has total financial control; Fatou has neither the document nor resources to move: "she had not seen her passport with her own eyes since she had arrived at the Derawal home, and she had been told from the start that her wages were to be retained by the Derawals to pay for the food and water and heat she would require during her stay, as well as to cover the rent for the room she slept in."[24]

Smith's story works stylistically to illuminate and interconnect two shadow worlds. Constructing her story with a seamless montage, she has the spaces and speculations about the two venues – the embassy and the household – flow together without significant pauses. And much of the imagery is about what is dark and/or hidden. For example in the pool where Fatou swims (lacking a proper bathing suit), she is "thankful for the semi-darkness in which [it] kept its clientele, as if the place were a nightclub, or a midnight Mass."[25] And the comings and goings of some of the people involved with the embassy are shrouded in mystery. On the one hand, there are the young tourist-trekkers, who obviously visit the embassy to obtain visas to engage in "dark tourism" (visits to the sites of atrocities),[26] but on the other, there is a Cambodian woman who is difficult to identify. Looking neither "like a New Person or an Old Person – neither clearly of the city nor of the country [Khmer Rouge modes of identification during their extermination campaign],"[27] she is seen by Fatou frequently exiting from the embassy, carrying bags that have no indication as to their content: "She had in her hands many bags from Sainsbury's [which] Fatou found a little mysterious: where was she taking all that shopping?...Fatou wondered whether they weren't in fact very old bags – hadn't their design changed?"[28]

Lest there be any doubt about the significance of a *Cambodian* embassy, Smith inserts a documentary statement:

"To keep you is no benefit. To destroy you is no loss" was one of the mottoes of the Khmer Rouge. It referred to the New People, those city dwellers who could not be made to give up city life and work on a farm...When a New Person was relocated from the city to the country, it was vital not to show weakness in the fields. Vulnerability was punishable by death.[29]

Near the end of the story, the Derawals dismiss Fatou from service, seemingly because after she rescues one of their choking children, they cannot face her. The Derawal's servant imaginary, in which Fatou has been located in a zone of indiscernibility between a person and thing, has been disrupted. Confronted with the arbitrariness of the order of their household, they first avert their eyes and then remove the body/person that threatens to expose their hierarchical allocation of personhood. Unable either to make eye contact with Fatou or to verbalize her and her husband's discomfort with Fatou's new status as one who has exited thingness by engaging in a non-servile act, Mrs Derawal's reason for the dismissal partakes of some of the same language as the Khmer Rouge's motto:

What you don't understand is that we have no need for a nanny...The children are grown. We need a housekeeper who cleans properly. These days you care more about the children than the cleaning...And that is no use to us.[30]

Smith's aesthetic strategy, a montage of heterogeneous elements which, using a common measure that connects the two venues of atrocity (including ultimately the elimination of people of "no use"), is a strategy that Jacques Rancière explicates in an analysis of Jean-Luc Godard's film *Histoire(s) du Cinema*. The film, according to Rancière, contains a "clash of heterogeneous elements that provide a common measure." It creates an equivalence between "two captivations,"[31] that of the "German crowds by Nazi ideology" and that of the "film crowds by Hollywood."[32] Clearly, the montage style of Smith's story is decidedly cinematic. The levels of experience it inter-articulates in London's life-world is reminiscent of a film that illuminates another relevant aspect of London, Stephen Frears' *Dirty Pretty Things* (2002). Inasmuch as the critical effect of Smith's "The Embassy of Cambodia" is its depiction of a shadow world of precarious lives, her story bears comparison with the London of Frears' film, which also reveals precarious lives that are not part of the iconic London available to either the diplomatic or touristic gaze.[33] In *Dirty Pretty Things*, the London venues we see are peripheral and shadowy – a hospital, a morgue, a sweatshop with rows of illegals sewing clothes, an immigrant-run private cab firm, an immigrant-run store selling exotic herbs, an underground car park, and a hotel basement.

In both Smith's story and Frears' film, London is simultaneously a destination for precarious bodies (the film opens and closes at Heathrow Airport) and a place where they are mistreated. The exploited and abused bodies in both are sequestered in buildings that segregate and hide the abuse (the Derawal's home in the story and the Baltic Hotel and a sweatshop in the film). The two abused and exploited characters in the film, a Turkish refugee, Senay (Audrey Tatou) and a Nigerian Doctor, Okwe (Chiwetel Ejiofor), who work in the hotel illegally as a chamber maid and desk clerk respectively (until Senay leaves the hotel for work in the sweatshop), are blackmailed into an organ harvesting scheme by the hotel's manager, Senior Juan, aka Sneaky (Sergi Lopez) because their illegal statuses render them vulnerable to arrest and deportation. The film's cuts and juxtapositions contrast the Baltic Hotel's lobby, where guests move freely in and out of the hotel, as they use the city as a space of enjoyment, with the hotel's management office, basement, and organ harvesting rooms, where the suborned employees are harassed by immigration inspectors and exploited by the hotel manager.

Because Senay and Okwe are in London as refugees, escaping atrocities in their home countries, Turkey and Nigeria respectively, *Dirty Pretty Things*, like "The Embassy of Cambodia," discloses a shadow world in the "first world," one that replicates the forms of violence that are more visible elsewhere. At the same time, in both the film and the story, there are spaces of reprieve where those with precarious lives find immigrant interlocutors who help them give voice to the atrocities they see and experience. In the case of the film, it's a morgue, where Okwe's Chinese mortician friend, Guo (Benedict Wong), engages him in a dialogue about his oppressed condition and ultimately helps him escape it. In the story, it's a Hungarian bakery, where Fatou's Nigerian friend, Andrew, engages her in dialogue about both her oppression and about notable global atrocities (and ultimately arranges to rescue her, once she is dismissed from the Derawal household).

The concept of a shadow world, which emerges from a critical encounter with those artistic genres helps me to structure Chapter 1, in which the primary contrast is between the visible venue of the war crimes trial and the shadowy exchanges in the world of arms trading, which create some of the conditions of possibility for war crimes and atrocities. And the highlighted spaces for dialogue about war, atrocity and justice in the story and film help me shape the last chapter (on justice and the archives), where I treat the spatial predicates of the voices of those involved in the construction of archives. More generally, throughout the chapters in this book, as concepts are mobilized in encounters with artistic texts, the method with which I analyze war crimes, atrocities and justice is (roughly speaking) what Cesare Casarino calls "philopoesis," which involves encounters between the concepts drawn from critical political and philosophical discourses and (artistic) texts. What results from such encounters, when a set of such concepts is deployed to "interfere" (Casarino's term, drawn from the cinema philosophy of Gilles Deleuze) with texts that are constituted as sets of affects and percepts, is critical political thinking.[34] Smith's protagonist Fatou in "The Embassy of Cambodia" provides a exemplary illustration for explicating the method. The embassy she passes can be construed as an "encountered sign."[35] She is affected by the encounter, begins to see her environment differently, and as a result begins to think about atrocities. Heeding Deleuze's concept of the encountered sign allows us to turn a story that at first appears to be merely experiential into a politically charged treatise; it makes us *think* about atrocities, where "thinking," as opposed to the mere recognition of established opinion or the extrapolation from established versions of facticity, requires conceptual innovation. I inaugurate that philopoetic method and the thinking it seeks to contribute with a brief review of some of the conceptual legacies of my inquiry here.

My investigations in this book are a legacy of two justice-themed chapters in my last set of inquiries, which was focused on aesthetic method.[36] In one chapter, "The Micropolitics of Justice," I analyze a Romanian film and an Italian crime novel, both of which stage encounters between legal justice apparatuses and embodied senses of justice. In the film, *Police Adjective* (2009), a police detective tries unsuccessfully to resist the policing and prosecutorial apparatuses and their discursive legitimations, which have assigned him a sting operation to catch and arrest youthful hashish users. In the novel, a prosecutor from Parma in the North of Italy tries unsuccessfully to try suspects in a murder case in Southern Italy, where he is defeated by the community's sense of justice, a structure of feeling that is resistant to the official legal codes of the state's justice system. My analysis in that chapter juxtaposes what I call the macro versus the micro politics of justice, where at a macro level, the politics of justice is about the state-level promulgation and administration of the law, and at the micro level it is about a politics of embodied affect, as both individuals and collectives develop sensibilities about the law and bring their coping strategies in response into discourse.

To provide a brief example of the juxtaposition, I repeat a quotation about one of the protagonists, an informer, in the crime novel, Leonardo Sciascia's *The Day of the Owl*:

> To the informer the law was not a rational thing born of reason, but something depending on a man, on the thoughts and the mood of the man here [Belodi, the prosecutor from the North]...The informer had never, could never have, believed that the law was definitely codified and the same for all; for him between rich and poor, between wise and ignorant, stood the guardians of the law who only used the strong arm on the poor; the rich they protected and defended.[37]

Inasmuch as such encounters reveal the contentiousness and situatedness of justice, here as throughout the book, I presume that it is unproductive to pose the question, "what is justice?" Instead, in accord with Gilles Deleuze's suggestion that, "Given any concept, we can always discover its drama,"[38] I pose questions of justice with a grammar that is sensitive to the historical staging of justice. Because both conceptually and as an object of affective commitment "justice" eventuates as an ongoing *drama of encounter*, the relevant questions are about when, where, how, from whose perspective(s), and under whose control it is activated as an issue and implemented through justice-related apparatuses.

The other justice-themed chapter providing a legacy for this inquiry is, "Zones of Justice," which is focused on the

protagonist in Mathias Énard's novel *Zone*, Francis Servain
Mirković, a French Croatian who had enlisted to fight in
the ethnic purification-driven Croatian independence war.
My emphasis in that chapter is on two aspects of Mirković
– how his movements map the spaces of justice and how
he evinces a plasticity as one who is involved in a process
of becoming (a reformed, Mirković narrates the novel
while on a train from Milan to Rome, holding an archive
of atrocities which he plans to sell to the Vatican). As
Mirković puts it at one point, "I'm changing my life my
body my memories my future my past."[39] The key moment
in the chapter is a scene in which Mirković reflects on his
impressions of the trial at the ICTY in The Hague of his
former Croatian commander, Blaškić. That scene is the
initiating inspiration for this investigation. It inaugurates
Chapter 1.

1

The Global Justice *Dispositif*

The Inspiration

Early in Mathias Énard's novel *Zone*, his protagonist,
Francis Servain Mirković, upon seeing his former commander, Blaškić, on trial at The Hague (a "multilingual
circus of the ICJ"), remarks, Blaškić is:

in his box at The Hague among the lawyers the interpreters
the prosecutors the witnesses the journalists the onlookers
the soldiers of the UNPROFOR who analyzed the maps
for the judges commented on the possible provenance of
bombs according to the size of the crater determined the
range of the weaponry based on the caliber which gave
rise to so many counter-arguments all of it translated into
three languages... everything had to be explained from the
beginning, historians testified to the past of Bosnia, Croatia,
and Serbia since the Neolithic era by showing how Yugoslavia was formed, then geographers commented on demo-
graphic statistics, censuses, land surveys, political scientists
explained the differential political forces present in the
1990s... Blaškić in his box is one single man and has to
answer for all our crimes, according to the principle of
individual criminal responsibility which links him to

history, he's a body in a chair wearing a headset, he is on trial in place of all those who held a weapon...[1]

In this remarkable reflection, Énard's Mirković, who is traveling from Milan to Rome with a suitcase containing an archive of atrocities committed in the Mediterranean zone, constructs a justice *dispositif,* where a *dispositif* is a complex ensemble of discourses, agencies, and apparatuses of implementation. The primary development of the concept belongs to Michel Foucault, who uses it variously. However in his most elaborate rendering, it is a "a thoroughly heterogeneous ensemble consisting of discourses, institutions, architectural forms, regulatory decisions, laws, administrative measures, scientific statements, philosophical, moral and philanthropic propositions...the said as much as the unsaid...the elements of the apparatus."[2] As it is manifested in the trial observed by Mirković, the *dispositif* involved represents the historical eventuation of a "will to know" in legal proceedings which, prior to the nineteenth century, was "*almost* entirely prescriptive."[3]

Gilles Deleuze's Foucault-inspired rendering of the *dispositif* adds crucial nuances to the concept. Beginning with three primary dimensions of Foucauldian analysis: "knowledge, power, and subjectivity,"[4] Deleuze emphasizes the mutations in the assemblages constituting a *dispositif* – for example those historical events that have shifted the "lines of force" involved in structures of command (over others and/or over oneself). And especially crucial for Deleuze are the changes in the apparatuses that govern or liberate "lines of subjectivation, lines of cracking, breaking and ruptures...,"[5] i.e., those events that have summoned different subjects and new configurations of power, control, and interpretive privilege. To take leave of such abstractions and give the concept direct historical relevance to the justice *dispositif* in Miković's observations about Blaškić's trial, I refer to the specific mutation that created the frame within which the post-Second-World-War Nuremberg war criminals were prosecuted.

The primary discursive condition of possibility for the Nuremberg war crimes trials was a new collective subject, "humanity." Inasmuch as the Nazi death apparatuses included extensive anthropological concepts, which constituted hierarchical versions of human nature (for example Alfred Hoche's notorious gloss on "life unworthy of life"),[6] a juridical response required a counter anthropology as part of the Nuremberg justice *dispositif*. For that, "the conceptual development of a notion of 'crimes against humanity'" was crucial, even though that new collective subject, "humanity as a whole," as an object of a crime fit uneasily within established legal discourse.[7] The notion of crimes against humanity actually pre-dated the pre-trial Nuremberg negotiations. It was originally evoked in 1906 by E. D. Morel in reference to the atrocities in the "The Congo Free State." In his *History of the Congo Reform Movement,* he refers to King Leopold II of Belgium's conduct in the Congo as "a great crime against humanity."[8] Although the concept failed to gain juridical traction through the first half the twentieth century, which witnessed like atrocities in many colonial possessions, the pre-trial Nuremberg deliberations firmly established it. That mutation in juridical discourse (an alteration in the process of subjectivation) that stemmed from the official recognition of crimes against humanity, created a legacy that was in evidence in the Blaškić trial observed by Mirković in Énard's novel.

However, while the ICTY (the International Tribunal for the former Yugoslavia) was enabled in principle by the concept of humanity as a whole, its more material supports were lacking. As Pierre Hazan points out, "since its creation, the ICTY has been an antilogy, the bearer of hopes and contradictions," for although it has been "an extraordinary laboratory for international law,"[9] it has been disenabled not only by political resistance from states but also from the UN, which allocated no funds for investigations and litigation, forcing administrators and jurists to seek outside funds (which the UN Office of Legal Affairs opposed).[10] Moreover, the Tribunal functioned within a glaring political contradiction. Those individuals whom prosecutors were attempting to put on trial for war crimes were important players in the Balkans peace process. Thus, when the US Secretary of State, Lawrence Eagleburger, urged that "Slobodan Milosevic the president of Serbia, Radovan Karadzic, the self-declared President of the Serbian Bosnian Republic, and general Radko Mladic, the commander of the Bosnia Serb military forces, must eventually explain whether they sought to ensure, as international law requires, that their forces complied with international law [All three were finally indicted and brought to the Hague to face charges]," the US mediators in Geneva were resistant because such prosecutions would undermine the peace process.[11] In short, the conflictual history of the founding and functioning of the ICTY reveals the "tension between *realpolitik* and justice,"[12] the irony of a glaring political contradiction between peace-seeking and justice-seeking. That contradiction was also apparent in the belated constituting and inadequate functioning of the UN/Cambodian War Crimes Tribunal, which had to operate in a "politicized and complicated juridical milieu,"[13] having been assembled in a post 9/11 era in which its primary funding sponsor, the US was ambivalent about the value of proceeding and was accordingly slow in providing support (The "Cambodian Justice Act" was passed by the US Congress in 1994, and the Tribunal didn't begin operating until 2009). And more recently, the International Criminal Court at The Hague, facing a conflict between justice and geopolitics, "agreed to special rules for any defendant who performs 'extraordinary' public duties at the highest national level."[14] Specifically, the court is deferring the war crimes trials of the President of Kenya – Uhuru Kenyatta and his deputy William Ruto (charged with orchestrating violence during the 2007 elections) – during the period of their public service.

As my analysis proceeds, I elaborate the war crimes-related justice *dispositif*, treating not only the moment that is addressed in the cited passage from Énard's novel at the beginning of this chapter (his Blaškić is an actual historical character who served time, eight plus years, in prison for war crimes) but also the complex apparatuses involved in the contemporary war crimes justice "circuses" and other relevant events (and non-events). However before providing that elaboration, I want to situate the part of my methodological approach that draws on the concept of the *dispositif.*

Eschewing "Universals"

Richard Rorty provides a compelling critique of the way that universalist philosophy conceives the problem of justice. "Universalist philosophers," he writes, "assume with Kant that all the logical space for moral deliberation is now available – that all the important truths about right and wrong can not only be stated but be made plausible in language ready to hand."[15] He adds, "Universalist moral philosophers think that the notion violation of human rights provides sufficient conceptual resources... [and] The typical universalist is a moral realist, someone who thinks that true moral judgments are *made* true by something out there in the world."[16] Displacing universalist philosophy with a version of pragmatism and criticizing a "representationalist account of knowledge,"[17] Rorty argues in favor of recognizing the contestability of beliefs and the historical complications involved in designating the relevant subjects, for example a stabilized notion of "personhood."

However, Rorty's substitution for universalism is ultimately philosophically and politically naïve. His "pragmatism" (in which truth is a matter of "shared beliefs") resists the realist and universalist notions of a distortion of reality but alights on a metaphor of "evolutionary development"[18] (applied to belief consensus) and at the same time privileges the pragmatism of John Dewey and others as more adequate than the "Nietzsche, Heidegger, Derrida, Foucault tradition." Yet it is precisely that "tradition" that offers powerful critiques of such evolutionary thinking. Rorty implies that the appropriate method for grasping a concept like justice is to heed the evolution of consensus, whereas Foucault, among others engages in historical inquiries that show how the contingent events through which regimes of truth and justice are radically altered reflect not a growing consensus but rather episodic alterations in the structures of power and authority that constitute and manage different kinds of subjects. In effect his anti universalism to the contrary, Rorty's contingency-denying developmental "consensus" restores universalism. It is a modern version of the ancient Greek assumption of a socially unifying normative consensus that reflects a transcendent natural order that instantiates and warrants consensus.

As is well known, the development of the concept of justice in Greek philosophy – running from Homer through Hesiod to Plato – begins with universals. Justice is derived from *Dike*, a Homeric term whose translation is controversial but roughly means a right or appropriate act that conforms to the society's normative order. And because the human normative order is presumed to derive from a trans-human order, conduct is right conduct insofar it is sanctioned by a logos and ethos that transcends actions within the life-world. The Greek word that most closely responds to the usage of the term justice (ever since) is *Dikaiosune*, which is "a Platonic term, [that] means something like our own word, Justice. It could mean also something like righteousness, but not as a process like Homeric *Dike* but as a personal possession, the having or doing of one's own."[19]

Crucially for purposes of contrast, the problem of justice for the Greeks emerges in a didactic context. Homer and Hesiod were instructors, albeit operating within different spheres of instruction, "agriculture and warfare respectively."[20] Foucault's approach to justice is critical rather than didactic. He focuses on apparatuses of implementation and the power structures those apparatuses serve.

Justice for Foucault is therefore conceived as the outcome of regulatory agencies and procedures. For example, speaking of the penalties emerging from juridical and policing apparatuses, he writes:

> Penalty would...appear to be a way of handling illegalities, of laying down the limits of tolerance, of giving free reign to some, of putting pressure on others, of excluding a particular section, of making another useful or neutralizing certain individuals and of profiting from others. In short, penalty does not simply 'check' illegalities; it 'differentiates' them. It provides them with a general 'economy'.[21]

Foucault's approach to justice presumes a radical shift in justice's ontological predicates. As he points out, reviewing justice's "foundation...its first word," as it was developed and applied in ancient Greece, "The decision of justice will have to be right (*juste*)"; it will have to function in accord with "the order of the world."[22] In contrast to the Greek ontology of justice, Foucault embraces a Nietzschean ontology of disorder in which, as he puts it, "We must not imagine that the world turns toward us a legible face which we have only to decipher; the world is not the accomplice of our knowledge."[23] It is an ontology that also emerges as a literary event on the American scene with the emergence of the "hardboiled" detective fiction of Dashiell Hammett. Whereas the older genre, familiar in the classic detective stories (for example Conan Doyle's Sherlock Holmes stories) "celebrated the victory of public knowledge and civic solidarity over the dangers of private desire...Hard-boiled crime fiction transformed that story by radicalizing its tensions...civil society can no longer contain private desire, public knowledge rarely trumps specialized expertise, and the idea of a common culture seems both profoundly appealing and ultimately unbelievable."[24]

That transformation, in which the social order is portrayed without any consensual normative transcendence that would provide a warrant, is especially apparent in Hammett's *The Maltese Falcon* (1930). In the midst of the crime drama, apropos of nothing in the narrative to that point, Hammett's detective, Sam Spade, tells his client, Bridgid O'Shaughnessy, who turns out to be the ultimate perpetrator of the crime, a parable about a man named Flitcraft who radically changes his life after a near death experience. It's a parable that renders the social order as radically contingent. As I put it elsewhere, Flitcraft realizes "that he lives in an unsponsored random world in which no normative order governs life."[25] To appreciate the implications for inquiry of Foucault's and Hammett's departure from the assumption of a universal normative order governing life-worlds, we have to heed Foucault's remarks about his resistance to universals, which distance him from traditional modes of political analysis.

In his lectures under the title of *The Birth of Biopolitics*, Foucault begins with some remarks on his "choice of method," which he summarizes as a radical break with traditional analyses of political concepts: "instead of deducing concrete phenomena from universals, or instead of starting with universals as an obligatory grid of intelligibility for certain concrete practices, I would like to start with the concrete practices and, as it were, pass these universals through the grid of these practices."[26] Implementing that method in an analysis of emerging governmentalities, Foucault refers to "the state" as "that which exists, but which does not yet exist enough," such that the practice involved in *Raison d'Etat* "places itself between a state presented as a given and a state presented as having to be constructed and built."[27] How is the state "constructed and built" through various practices?

One of the more cogent analytic frames Foucault develops to treat that process of construction is in his discussion of the appropriate question for situating a "new programming of liberal governmentality," where he refers to "an internal reorganization that ... does not ask the state what freedom it will leave to the economy," but asks the economy how its freedom can have a state-creating function and role, in the sense that "it will really make possible the foundation of the state's legitimacy."[28] Heeding Foucault's epistemological analytic, the questions to pose in light of Énard's description of the practices surrounding the war crimes tribunal are about *how* "justice" is activated (becomes what it is) through such practices, and as well how states are (re)made as they are both legitimated and to some extent attenuated as justice is created and implemented, both within states and on an extra-state global scale.

Such a questioning accords with Foucault's analysis of the effects of the rule of law on the state form, where he points out that juridical institutions and military and policing practices emerged first to enhance royal power against feudal powers and subsequently attenuated royal discretionary power to serve an emerging *Raison d'Etat*.[29] As he enquires into the grid of intelligibility that historically attends the shaping of the state, Foucault concludes that ultimately, "The state is nothing else but the mobile effect of a regime of multiple governmentalities," where governmentalities are complex structures of strategic enactment that include "correlative institutions": diplomatic, policing and military, among others,[30] which are effectively sovereignty apparatuses (*dispositifs*). In short, Foucault doesn't begin with the state as a universal phenomenon and ask how it acts but instead inquires into how various enactments have created what constitutes the mobile, constantly changing phenomenon known as the state.

William Connolly offers a similar insight in his analysis of "the complexity of sovereignty." After noting that a democratic ethos, which is supposedly implemented through regulations and their implementations that purport to guarantee the sovereignty of the people, "circulates uncertainly between the multitude, the traditions it embodies, constitutionally sanctioned authorities and, where operative, the written constitution that the authorities interpret," he points to the vagaries of the apparatuses of implementation:

> The relative weight of each element can be specified more closely, although never completely, according to need and context. The police in American cities thus both express and help to shape the ethos of sovereignty. They can find evidence or plant it, follow the spirit of Miranda or render it ineffective, intimidate a section of the populace or act evenhandedly, depending on the unstable confluence of legal rulings given to them, the large ethos in which they participate, and the professional police ethos carved out of dangers, ethnic loyalties and hostilities in the city.[31]

In accord with Foucault's methodological injunction, Connolly is not beginning with the universal, "the sovereignty of the people," but rather with the practices though which such sovereignty is implemented as a mobile phenomenon, activated in part by the way policing operates as a segment of a popular sovereignty-making apparatus or *dispositif*.

Such approaches to the "state" (in Foucault's case) and popular sovereignty (in Connolly's) are not explicative; they are not aimed at finding a *cause*. Rather, they seek to make intelligible the ongoing practices that constitute and continuously reactivate those universals: states and sovereignty respectively.[32] To apply such an approach to what I am calling "the global justice *dispositif*," as it is disclosed in the fictional Mirković's long reflection, I want to heed another of Foucault's conceptual contributions to his method, what he calls "regimes of veridiction." Drawing on his investigation into the history punishment, he refers to the relationships between jurisdictional and veridictional practices, suggesting that what is to be revealed is "how a certain practice of veridiction was formed and developed in...penal institutions."[33] Lest that remark be taken to accord with Rorty's above-noted "evolutionary development," we should recall that modern "penal institutions" emerged as an abrupt historical event, a reversal in which what had been visible (punishment) became hidden while what had been hidden (the trial) became visible. As public executions disappeared, the trial, which had been formerly hidden, became the public spectacle and operated with a very different approach to punishment: "From art of unbearable sensation, punishment became an economy of suspended rights."[34]

However Foucault's most concrete illustrations of his concept of truth-as-veridictional practice are articulated in his inquiries into the history of medical discourse. For example, "I think that what is currently politically important is to determine the regime of veridiction established at a given moment that is precisely the one on the basis of which...doctors said so many stupid things about sex. What is important is the regime of veridiction that enabled them to say and assert a number of things as truths..."[35]

As is the case with his resistance to beginning with universals, in the process of mapping what he refers to as a history of regimes of veridiction, Foucault is not providing an explanation. As he has put it elsewhere, his critiques do not "partake of...so-called explicative procedures to which are attributed causal value..."[36] Instead, he is involved in "the critique of knowledge," which "consists in determining under what conditions and with what effects a veridiction is exercised."[37]

Without using the concept, Énard effectively describes, in a further observation, the regime of veridiction that enables what can and should be said (and by whom) at Blaškić's war crimes trial. His protagonist, Mirković, says:

> ...in the Great Trial organized by the international lawyers immersed in precedents and the jurisprudence of horror, charged with putting some order into the law of murder, with knowing at one instant a bullet in the head was a legitimate *de jure* and at what instant it constituted a grave breach of the law and customs of war...[38]

In contrast to Foucault's explicit narration of his method, Énard's analysis proceeds through juxtaposition, through "literary montage" (Walter Benjamin's method as noted in the Introduction) in which he shows rather than explicitly saying. Thus at one point in the novel, Mirković observes some of his fellow passengers on the train to Rome:

> Egyptian, Lebanese, and Saudi businessmen all educated in the best British and American prep schools, discreetly elegant, far from the clichés of colorful, rowdy Levantines, they were neither fat nor dressed up as Bedouins, they spoke calmly of the security of their future investments, as they said, they spoke of our dealings, of the region they called "the area," the zone, and the word "oil"...some had sold weapons to Croats in Bosnia, others to Muslims.[39]

In the context of Mirković's prior observation about Blaškić, who as "one single man...has to answer for all our crimes, according to the principle of individual criminal responsibility which links him to history," it is evident that the weapons dealers Mirković is observing and overhearing play a major, albeit unacknowledged role in the archive of the atrocities contained in his suitcase. They are unindicted, predatory entrepreneurs, functioning in a world in which global capitalism is redrawing the map as it secures its various clienteles, profiting from global antagonisms, ethno-national among others. Displaying no national or cultural emblems, these train passengers are without territorial allegiance. They have no explicit attitudes about who should be allowed to live and who should die. Nevertheless their conduct is "necropolitical;"[40] many fates are determined by a network of such amoral, predatory types, who aid and abet a violence that is in part a consequence of their conduct rather than a result of any explicit antagonistic intentions. As Mirković adds, "our businessmen from the Zone didn't see the threat behind the outstretched hand, the deadly games that would play out in the course of the years to come..."[41] These "businessmen" are able to ply their trade with relative impunity because they take advantage of a juridical map that bears a striking resemblance to the global cell phone map. Just as there exist many "dead zones," where receiving and sending phone communication cannot take place, there are many places where law is virtually non-existent.

To treat the consequences of such a juridical cartography, I turn first to the juridical/spatial conditions of possibility for arms trafficking and then to a primary analytic of this chapter, clashing cartographies – disjunctive relations among geopolitical security maps that respond to reasons of state, arms transfer maps involving both states and private entrepreneurs, juridical space (The Hague and other war crimes trail venues), the networks of policing agencies (Interpol's interconnections with other policing groups, for example the CIA and DEA), the map of peacekeeping operations, the map of sex trafficking (a practice that serves a "peacekeeping clientele" among others), and the entanglements of all of these with finance- and mediascapes. Indeed, the cartographic alterations stemming from emerging financescapes are especially crucial. As the novelist Michel Houellebecq observes in his *The Map and the Territory*: "…free-market economics redrew the geography of the world in terms of the expectations of the clientele, whether the latter moved to indulge in tourism or to earn a living. The flat isometric surface of the map was substituted by an abnormal topography where Shannon was closer to Katowice than to Brussels, to Fuerteventura than to Madrid."[42]

Another justice-related mapping, which has critical interrelationships with other mappings, emerges if we heed what I will call a global audiography – the sites from which atrocities are called to account in official statements. For example in July 2013, *The New York Times* reported that "The White House" was notably silent while the Egyptian military was involved in mass killings of Egyptian protesters.[43] It would appear that Egypt's strategic importance for US strategic interests in the region was trumping humanitarian concerns. To cite an earlier example, back in September of 2001, when the US had established a base in Uzbekistan from which to attack the Taliban in Afghanistan, and subsequently was using Uzbekistan as a surrogate jailer for "terrorist" suspects, the US became embarrassed by its "ally." "In the early spring of 2004, after a series of suicide bombings in Tashkent killed 47 people, many of them Uzbek police officers, the government cracked down against people on religious grounds, setting off international condemnation," and "three months later...the State Department said it would cut $18 million in military and economic aid to Uzbekistan because of its failure to improve its human rights record."[44] However just one month later the Chairman of the Joint Chiefs, General Richard B. Myers, announced that an additional $21 million in aid would be coming from the Pentagon to help the Uzbeks get rid of their biological weapon stockpile, and when it was pointed out that aid had been withheld because of the awful human rights record of the Uzbeks (e.g. torture consisting of boiling body parts), General Myers said that the United States had "benefited greatly from our partnership and strategic relationship with Uzbekistan," and that "in my view, we shouldn't let any single issue drive a relationship with any single country."[45] As I've put it elsewhere, "apparently the violence-by-proxy that the Uzbeks supply trumps US official concern with human rights."[46] This is yet another example of the disjunctive cartographies – in this case a clash between the audiography of voiced human rights concerns and the map of geopolitical interests, where the latter mutes voices and compromises justice. Moreover, implicated in the global audiography is the extant "media ecology" – for example the alternatively active and repressed practices of photo journalism, whose witnessing plays an important role in enabling the work of justice-related NGOs, thereby determining which kinds of atrocities in which places receive global attention.[47]

What I am suggesting therefore is that "justice" emerges from heterogeneous encounters within disjunctive spaces of engagement, where those "spaces" manifest a complex transversality, which the term "disjunctive" does not adequately cover. For example, there is a paradoxical effect

MISSIONS DIRECTED BY THE DEPARTMENT OF PEACEKEEPING OPERATIONS

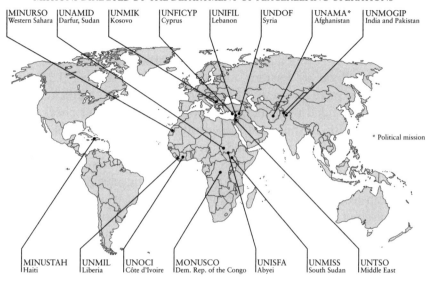

MINURSO	United Nations Mission for the Referendum in Western Sahara	established 1991
MINUSTAH	United Nations Stabilization Mission in Haiti	established 2004
MONUSCO	United Nations Organization Stabilization Mission in the Dem. Republic of the Congo	established 2010
UNAMA	United Nations Assistance Mission in Afghanistan	established 2002
UNAMID	African Union - United Nations Hybrid Operation in Darfur, Sudan	established 2007
UNDOF	United Nations Disengagement Observer Force	established 1974
UNFICYP	United Nations Peacekeeping Force in Cyprus	established 1964
UNIFIL	United Nations Interim Force in Lebanon	established 1978
UNISFA	United Nations Interim Security Force for Abyei	established 2011
UNMIK	United Nations Interim Administation in Kosovo	established 1999
UNMIL	United Nations Mission in Liberia	established 2003
UNMISS	United Nations Mission in the South Sudan	established 2011
UNMOGIP	United Nations Military Observer Group in India and Pakistan	established 1949
UNOCI	United Nations Operation in Côte d'Ivoire	established 2004
UNTSO	United Nations Truce Supervision Organization	established 1948

Image 1: UN Peacekeeping Operations

of official peacekeeping. The apparent stasis of this map (Image 1) of the UN Department of Peacekeeping Operations deployed around the globe is belied by the adverse mobilizing effect its has.

Wherever sizable peacekeeping forces are sent, sex traffickers begin capturing and trafficking women to provide them with sexual services. Peacekeeping, which is undertaken to prevent war crimes, has the effect of encouraging them. Thus, ironically, the map of peacekeeping induces a dynamic map of sex trafficking. For example, in the case of the peacekeepers in the former Yugoslavia, UN officials have aided and abetted sex trafficking: "The Associated Press in Eastern Europe has reported that [UN] officers have [secretly] forged documents for trafficked women, aided their illegal transport through order checkpoints into Bosnia, and tipped off sex club owners ahead of raids."[48] More generally, sex trafficking is, "A US$8 billion/year global business…It prostitutes almost four million girls and boys daily [and] Crime cartels utilize high-tech equipment, including weapons of war to defend this lucrative trade."[49] The sex trafficking aspect of war crimes and atrocities deserves further investigation. It has gotten broad publicity as a result of a feature film, *The Whistleblower* (2010), which is based on the experience of Kathryn Bolkovac (reported in her book by the same title), a Lincoln Nebraska police officer, who took a job with a private military contractor, DynaCorp, operating in Bosnia after the war. When she started investigating sex trafficking, she discovered that the clientele was the peacekeeping force, the IPTF (International Police Task Force).[50] Despite her whistleblowing in which she reported the atrocities (known and ignored by a special Representative of the UN Secretary General in Bosnia), neither the clientele nor the complicit officials at DynaCorp or in the UN were prosecuted because they had immunity. In effect postwar Bosnia contained a complex juridical cartography. Contractors and peacekeepers constituted a juridical void that followed them like a "little halo" wherever they were. Their presence produced a mobile non-juridical space within juridical space. However, here I raise the issue primarily to complicate the concept of cartographic intersections. Although there is a critical interaction between sex trafficking and arms trading, my focus in what follows is on the relationship between arms trading and spaces of justice, where there are also juridical voids.

"Disarming Viktor Bout"

The "Egyptian, Lebanese, and Saudi businessmen," on Mirković's train in Énard's *Zone* have an exemplary real-life counterpart in the career of Viktor Bout ("distinguished [in the eyes of "officials" in Washington] not by cruelty or ruthlessness but by cunning amorality"),[51] who was sentenced to twenty-five years for arms trafficking in a New York court in February 2012. A Russian entrepreneur who began his arms trafficking business in the early 1990s, Bout's remark about one of his first places of business is pregnant with implications for understanding the spaces of justice. Early in his arms trafficking career, he lived in and operated from Sharjah in the United Arab Emirates ("a kind of postmodern caravansary") because, as he told a reporter, it was a place with "practically no law."[52]

Bout's strategy, which takes advantage of an uneven juridical global cartography, is strikingly parallel to the way HBO's Deadwood series (3 seasons, 2004–6) begins by observing the US's nineteenth century juridical cartography in the American West. In the first episode of season one, a main protagonist, Seth Bullock (Timothy Oliphant), a Marshall in the Montana Territory, decides after dealing with the difficulties of law enforcement to move to the town of Deadwood in the Dakota Territory, where he says, "there's no law at all" to open a hardware store. In the Deadwood of post 1876, legal apparatuses had yet to be institutionalized. Neither violence nor business ventures were significantly inhibited by law enforcement.

Doubtless the "wild west" model still fits much of the global scene. Juridical space contains many "gray zones" (one of Viktor Bout's favorite types of venue). Legally speaking (the literal meaning of jurisdiction"), "war crimes are limited to situations of international armed conflict," and according to the 1949 Geneva Convention, international tribunals can only prosecute individuals who perpetrate a "grave breach committed against a person protected by the Convention."[53] That excludes many people from the population of protected juridical subjects and leaves many amoral commercial predators free to supply the weapons that wreak havoc. With respect to commerce, many places – e.g., Sharjah where Bout launched the airfreight business he ultimately used to transfer arms – exist outside of global trade regulation laws and their implementing apparatuses.

The American West, realistically depicted in the *Deadwood* series, was also "wild" in that policing was unevenly distributed and ambiguously tasked. There was little or no institutionalized coordination among territorial Marshalls, local sheriffs, army commands, and private armies (for example the Pinkertons, who performed security and policing functions for hire). The global policing scene is similarly wild. The policing agencies of various states – for example the FBI, CIA, DEA, NSA, and ATF agencies of the US – are loosely coordinated by Interpol, an intergovernmental organization whose role is to coordinate responses to both violent and commercial crimes that operate across borders. However, while Interpol is an allegedly neutral organization, some have observed that it tends to target certain nationals and ignore others. In order to treat the policing aspect of the justice *dispositif*, I turn here to two episodes of policing agency collaboration, the apprehension of Bout in Thailand, and the arrest of members of the "Pink Panthers," a worldwide jewelry theft gang.

Bout's arrest in Thailand involved a long-planned policing collaboration. He was apprehended by Thai police who were working with the DEA, a "crime-fighting" agency whose major target has been drug crimes but "had begun to prove that it could go after veritable untouchables and bring them to justice, for example their arrest of Monzer al-Kassar, a Syrian arms trafficker living in Spain."[54] As was the case with their arrest of al-Kassar, the DEA set up a sting to capture Bout. They used suborned informants who posed as Colombian FARC operatives in the market for anti-aircraft missiles to use against the American helicopters that were helping the Colombian government's campaign against FARC. The DEA's sting involved not only the use of a cooperating policing network but also (ironically like Bout) the exploitation of the uneven juridical map. For example, they tried first to set up the sting in Romania because "they knew that local authorities would let them tap phones."[55] The map of the DEA's sting operation was extensive; for example it included not only Colombia but also the Congo. (One suborned informant, a Congo-based businessman was used to help set up the Thailand meeting).

Although it took two years, the DEA sting was consummated when a Thai court approved Bout's extradition to the US, where he was tried and convicted. Recalling that the DEA is supposed to be about drug trafficking, their involvement in the Bout sting reveals not only their expansive geography of operation but also the expansion of their role. With the diminution of battlefronts, as the US has increasingly functioned in zones of violence where the line between war- and crime-fighting is increasingly ambiguous, the DEA has become a virtual paramilitary force. For example, a militarized DEA accompanied police in a proxy war in Honduras: "Pursuing a boatload of cocaine smugglers," they "opened fire on another boat carrying villagers, killing four people" ("including two pregnant women") and wounding four others. The euphemistic designation of the militarized DEA "commando squads" is the acronym FAST ("Foreign-deployed Advisory Support Team").[56]

What does the Honduran attack by the DEA say about the vagaries of that part of the "justice *dispositif*" best termed the new war *dispositif*? Given that in the "war on drugs" and the "war on terror," conventional warfare is being displaced by what Gregoire Chamayou terms "the doctrine of the manhunt," militarized policing agencies have become more involved than traditional "armed services."[57] For example, the CIA is "no longer a traditional espionage service devoted to stealing the secrets of foreign governments...[instead it] has become a killing machine, an organization consumed with man hunting."[58] The shift away from the wars with clear battlefronts, "manned" by the armed services, to "cynegetic war, armed violence [that] seeks to pursue the prey wherever it might be...[and where] the place of hostilities is no longer defined by the locatable space of an effective combat zone, but by the simple presence of the hunted individual who carries with him everywhere a kind of little halo denoting a personal hostility zone,"[59] has implications for war crimes. In cynegetic war, policing agencies are not prepared or inclined to heed the various protocols in place (the Uniform Code of Military Justice, The Geneva Convention, and other "laws of war")[60] to protect noncombatants. "Juridically" speaking, "formally distinguishing between combatants and civilians is known as the *principle of distinction*...a peremptory obligation of international humanitarian law...[however] the principle of distinction, taken on its own terms, has proved to be remarkably frail. Contemporary armed conflicts, marked by a 'mixture of war, crime and human rights violations,' are nasty, brutish, and increasing in duration and devastation."[61]

Moreover, the violations are enabled by the contemporary forms of enmity as well as by the new war technologies involved. There is a new and different cartography of enmity ("a shadow war waged across the globe [in which] America has pursued its enemies using killer robots and special-operations troops"),[62] which, like the cartography of arms transfers, contributes different problems of atrocity and justice. To illuminate the complexities of cartographies of illicit enterprises and the policing practices they provoke, I turn to an encounter between a jewelry theft enterprise and the global policing *dispositif*, which operates against the jewelry theft network as well as against other forms of illicit trade.

Apprehending Pink Panthers

Inasmuch as Viktor Bout's "crimes" were both commerce-and war-related, before elaborating the disjunctive carto-graphic networks within which his enterprise was situated, I want to go back to the fallout from the breakup of the former Yugoslavia (which yielded a Blaškić) and treat an episode of global crime fighting that involved Serbian, Croatian and Montenegrin perpetrators, because it shows how the "grid of intelligibility" I refer to as the global justice *dispositif* is as much in evidence with respect to commercial crimes as it is to war crimes. David Samuels' investigation of the apprehension of some members of a global jewelry theft gang, "the Pink Panthers," begins with a scene at the high-end jewelry franchise, Graff's flagship store on Bond Street in London, being cased by a Mon-tenegrin member of the gang, Pedrag Vujosevic from Bijea. Later, he is joined in a heist of the store by another Mon-tenegrin, Milan Jovetic, from Cetinje and by Nebosja Denic, "a hulking Serb from Kosovo," assisted by Jovetic's Serbian girlfriend, Ana Stankovic.[63]

Why so many jewelry thieves from the former Yugosla-via? As Samuels point out:

> Criminal gangs became dominant forces in Serbia during the Balkan conflicts of the 1990s, and they were further empowered by Western sanctions, which gave them a stranglehold on the markets for gasoline, cigarettes, and other staples. After Slobodan Milosevic became president in 1989, smuggling operations directed by the Serb state pumped billions of dollars into the bank accounts of politi-cal elites... 'Milosevic, apart from being a very brutal auto-crat, essentially criminalized the state completely.'[64]

To put the observation in Foucault's methodological frame, in the case of Serbia under Milosevic, the "state" was in part constituted by crime.[65] As Samuels notes, "Once the Serbian state had transformed itself into a criminal enterprise, many Serbs turned themselves, willingly or reluctantly, into criminals." There is a compelling connection between "Milosevic's wars" and the production of crime. After the war had decimated the police force ("fifteen cops out of fifty got themselves killed in Croatia and Bosnia"), the state released felons to add to the bodies on the front lines, and "those who survived were allowed to remain at large."[66]

In addition to the war-related production of thieves are other structural conditions of possibility for the Panther's crime spree. Rife inequality all over the planet produces the wealth of consumers who can support jewelry stores like Graff's (whose clients "include Oprah Winfrey and Victoria Beckham") and Choppard's, whose Tokyo location was hit by the Panthers when they exploited a visit by the wife of the French Prime Minister Jean-Pierre Raffarin (netting them fourteen million dollars worth of jewels from an unguarded display case)."[67] Other contributing conditions include the artificial control over diamonds by the Belgian companies, who control the supplies, and the various crafts that help turn them into commodities (for example Ivy Cutler a diamond grader, working in the Gemological Institute of America in New York).

The habitus of high-end consumption also contributes because the jewelry stores catering to the wealthy tend to avoid a high level of visibly manned security, lest it turn off their clientele. As a result, the security response has to rest with a global policing network: private detectives, police personnel from various nations, and the coordinating work of Interpol. Thus in one episode of the coordination of the apprehension of Pink Panthers, Interpol alerted the Monaco police about the whereabouts of two key members of the gang. They pursued the Bosnian, Dusko Poznan, and the Serb, Borko Ilincic as they passed Place du Casino and several jewelry stores before being captured by a camera outside one of them (Zegg and Cerlati). They were subsequently caught in Princess Grace Hospital after

Poznan was purposely hit by a police operative's car and accepted medical assistance.

As the judicial machinery ground on at the time of Samuels' investigation (2007), Poznan was extradited to Liechtenstein and Ilincic was put on trial in Switzerland. Another Pink Panther, the Serb, Milan Ljepoja, famous for a spectacular heist in Dubai and responsible for a Liechtenstein jewelry heist as well, also fell prey to inter-police agency cooperation and was arrested on the Swiss-French border, largely through the detective work of Yan Glassey of Geneva.[68]

"Robbing a Bank's No Crime Compared to Owning One."

To return to Foucault's methodological practice: Rather than treating "crime" as a universal and inquiring into its causes, I want to note the complex policing and diplomacy practices that constitute much of the crime *dispositif*, determining what forms of theft get treated as crime waves and what illicit commercial practices, pervasive though they may be, attract little or no policing (and in fact tend to get free passes by the various agencies of the state system). While the Pink Panther's take from jewelry stores in recent years is in the millions, their haul pales in comparison with the illegal commerce of large global corporations. In recent years, the trend in global commerce is toward the expansion of "shadow markets," which result when large corporations turn to "small, illegal, off-the-books businesses for trillions of dollars in commerce [which now] employ fully half the world's workers."[69] That figure comes from an analysis of the black and gray markets in which corporations evade taxation by selling their products through street vendors around the world rather than by establishing store outlets. An analyst who has investigated this trend, Robert Neuwirth, is in effect part of the journalistic contribution to the "crime" *dispositif* (contributing to what gets constituted as crime) in that he claims that although the commerce "flies under the radar of government [and is thus] unregistered, unregulated, untaxed [it is not] outright criminal – I don't include gun-running, drugs, human trafficking, or things like that."[70]

As for some of the players: Proctor and Gamble "hires a local distributor – sometimes several layers of local distributors – to get [their products] from a legal, formal, tax paying company to a company willing to deal with unlicensed vendors who don't pay taxes."[71] Similarly, the cell phone company MTN, upon discovering that setting up a mobile phone market in Third World countries like the ones in Britain or the US didn't result in significant profits, "retooled" and sold phone cards through street vendors, reaping profits of "around $2.4 Billion in Nigeria alone."[72] The cartography of such "shadow economies" is disjunctive with the geopolitical power security/antagonism map as well as with a cartography of policing controls. Although the street market economy accounts for close to 50 percent of exchanges in China (as is the case with much of Africa), it accounts for only around 10 percent of such exchanges in the US. In short, the global map of shadow economies indicates the extent to which global capital-as-extended-"crime spree," functions outside of the politics of security (and with relative impunity).

Another "Shadow World"

At both his extradition trial in Bangkok and his criminal trial in New York, Viktor Bout's attorney complained about the jury-biasing effect of Andrew Niccol's feature film, *Lord of War* (2005), in which the story of the main protagonist, the arms trader, Yuri Orlov (Nicholas Cage), is based on the life of Viktor Bout. One image (what André Bazin famously refers to as an "image-fact")[73] is exemplary because it articulates a post-cold war global reality.

Image 2: Viktor Orlov with Lenin

Showing a cold war figure being displaced by a war-related commercial one, Orlov (as the Bout surrogate) is sitting in an outdoor armaments depot in a Russian republic, next to a toppled statue of Lenin, as he works his hand-held calculator (Image 2). In the background is a line of idle tanks he is planning to buy in order to supply one side in a war. The ideological basis of violent contention is being replaced by the cynical, commercial assistance to it.

Throughout the film, Niccol's cinematic cartography is faithful to the map of Viktor Bout's arms trading enterprise, and the viewer is prepared to see the cartographic basis of the Orlov/Bout story, for the film begins with cartographic imagery. Before the credits are run, the screen is filled with a Kalashnikov rifle, superimposed on a schematic map of the globe.

That shot prepares us for the film's articulation of an arms sale mapping, for, as Tom Conley points out in his treatment of cinematic cartography, "It can be said that in its first shots a film establishes a geography with which every spectator is asked to contend."[74] Once the plot develops, the film's mapping of Orlov's arms acquisitions and sales closely matches most of those of Viktor Bout – buying idle weapons in the post-Soviet Russian republics and selling them in The Middle East, Latin America (Cartagena), Africa (Liberia, Sierra Leone, and The Ivory Coast) and Afghanistan. And crucially, apart from what it depicts, the film goes on to become part of the mediascape that testifies to the amorality of arms trades accomplished by a man who, like the characters on Mirković's train, has no interest in who is targeted by what he sells.

The arms sales enterprise of Viktor Bout has a legacy that includes not only individual entrepreneurs – for example the early twentieth century arms dealer, Basil Zaharoff, a Turk who provided "the template for those who followed him"[75] – but also many states: "The US, Russia, France, Germany, Sweden, Holland, Italy, Israel, and China are regularly identified as the largest producers and traders of weapons and materiel ["equipment, apparatus, and supplies of a military force"]."[76] However, the consolidating term "states" is misleading because the weapons they sell are products of multiple-state commodity production. For example the "American-made" F-16 jet fighter plane, a global best seller, contains "high-tech components from Germany, Israel, Japan, and Russia," and its assembly is outsourced to various global sites. In general, as Ann Markusen points out, "Arms manufacturers are following the lead of their commercial counterparts and going global, pursuing transnational mergers, and marketing operations abroad."[77] As a result of the mergers, which bring together entities with different maps of friends versus foes, the clientele for sales emerge from diverse, often conflicting security topographies (adding to the disjunctive relationship between security and commodity sales cartographies). For example, there is the "Pentagon's New Map,"[78] which differentiates states on the basis of their American capitalism-friendly susceptibilities."[79] At the same time, as a result of the arms production mergers, the Pentagon, a client for arms, has decreasing control over where "US" weapons end up. As Feinstein puts it, "The arms industry and its powerful political friends have forged a parallel

Why just calling it a shadow world counts to me obliquely

The Global Justice _Dispositif_ 39

political universe that largely insulates itself against the influence or judgment of others by invoking national security. This is a shadow world."[80] And as was the case with Viktor Bout's "shadow world," that universe's victims are as likely to perish because of the pursuit of economic advantage as they are from structured inter-state antagonisms, or at times from a combination of the two. One such example derives from the need for weapons to be field-tested on a live adversary to be sold to the Pentagon. There was an episode in the post Vietnam (but still cold war) era, when a veteran Vietnam War helicopter pilot was hired by a group comprised of US and South African military personnel, Pentagon officials, and representatives of a weapons manufacturer to drop their new product, incendiary bombs, on Marxist rebels in Namibia.[81]

What are the implications of such economic, security, and other clashing cartographies for war crimes-related global justice? Bout's crimes, and his insensitivity to the lives his weapons deals ended up extinguishing, bear comparison with those of many state-sponsored forms of arms sales. Without going into an extensive survey, I want to point to one episode, which the journalist Bill Moyers termed "High Crimes and Misdemeanors," the Iran-Contra affair in which the US traded weapons to Iran (100 US Tow missiles sold through Israel) in exchange for the release of hostages in Lebanon, and, at the same time, illegally armed the Nicaraguan "Contras by using funds solicited from foreign leaders (for example, the King of Saudi Arabia).[82] That "criminal gang," like the Pink Panthers, operated through several global locations. Congressional hearings ended with prosecutions of lower level functionaries (one CIA operative was convicted of felonies) but failed to lead to an impeachment process, and in 1992 President George H. M. Bush pardoned the conspirators, from Defense Secretary Casper Weinberger on down. And, as Moyer's documentary reveals, the arms sent to Nicaragua took innocent lives without a "war crime" issue gaining traction in the US or elsewhere.

"Justice" in and from the Balkans War

To return to the inspiration, the trial of Blaškić, the legacies of the Balkans War are diverse. On the one hand are the above-noted criminal gangs – various indicted and prosecuted war criminals from Serbia, Croatia and Bosnia – and on the other are writers and filmmakers (both exilic and domestic), whose works continually reinflect the will-have-been of the Balkans War. With respect to the war crimes legacy, the ongoing trials at The Hague Tribunal testify to the limitations under which legal justice functions. Making the above-noted Blaškić's fate seem arbitrary, on May 30, 2013 the Tribunal acquitted two Serbian "security officials," Jovica Stanisic and Franko Simatovic, who "had the largest hand in creating, training, arming, financing and directing several of the paramilitary groups responsible for a large number of crimes in Croatia and Bosnia-Herzegovina."[83] The reasoning of the justices is telling with respect to the vagaries of legal justice as it applies to war crimes:

> Although the chamber affirms that a joint criminal enterprise to create ethnically homogeneous populations existed, it rejects the theory that concrete contributions to the realization of this enterprise by themselves constitute guilt. Instead it applies a standard that demands a type of evidence that no major criminals have ever produced in any conflict: documentation indicating specific instructions that crimes be committed. The narrowness of the standard is suggested by a baffling sentence in the verdict: the tribunal's majority "considers Stanisic's reference to killings and his remark that 'we'll exterminate them completely' to be too vague to be construed as support for the allegation that Stanisic shared the intent to further the alleged common criminal purpose."[84]

Those judgments, along with the fact that the ICTY at The Hague has limited powers – only signatories to the statute creating the Court can have their citizens tried by the tribunal – point to the severe limitations of legal justice. Although there are other courts within the global justice cartography, at most they play symbolic roles in which, as part of the justice mediascape, they expose other perpetrators and other victims, while at the same time creating spaces in which to reflect on justice/injustice. They participate in the imaginative practices that constitute how justice is conceived. There is for example The BRussells Tribunal in Kuala Lumpur, where war crimes charges were brought against President George W. Bush and Associates, and there is the Spanish Judge Baltasar Garzon, who has brought charges of terrorism and genocide against various persons and organizations – attempting for example to prosecute the former Chilean President, Augusto Pinochet for human rights abuses.[85]

However, in the concluding section of this chapter, my emphasis is on a part of the mediascape I am designating as a literary cartography in which the participants are writers, exilic Bosnians (among others) and a Bosnian filmmaker. Their efforts constitute what (after the distinction developed by Shoshana Felman) I refer to as "literary justice." As she points out, in contrast to the "legal justice," dispensed at trials ("physical theaters of justice"), "Literature is a dimension of concrete embodiment and a language of infinitude that in contrast to the language of the law, encapsulates not closure but precisely what in a given legal case refuses to be closed and cannot be closed. It is to this refusal of the trauma to be closed that literature does justice."[86]

There are two post Balkans War streams; one is a flow of persons into exile – what Dubravka Ugrešić (a Croatian émigré living in Amsterdam) refers to as "the Balkans Express"[87] – and the other into the Hague to be tried for war crimes. Although the former would appear more virtuous than the latter, many of them, though not formally on trial, indict themselves (often having a sense of being divided selves) for fleeing and leaving family and friends behind to cope with the dangers of the war. To situate the two venues: The spaces of exile summon the texts of exilic writers from the Balkans and produce a "literary justice," while the spaces of tribunals (primarily the ICTY in the Hague but there are other locations, as I have noted) are spaces of "legal justice." While the former is exceedingly broad in scope and resistant to closure, the latter is exceedingly narrow, hemmed in by the nuances of evidence and complex concepts of agency and influence and forced to end in definitive (and often unsatisfying) judgments.

What role has literature played in exposing and continually rehearsing and reflecting on the war crimes in the Balkans? To begin to answer that question, I refer first to Steven Galloway's novel *The Cellist of Sarajevo*, which mobilizes diverse aesthetic subjects (city inhabitants who resist attempts to kill the city), among whom is a cellist who is based on an actual historical personage, Vedran Smailovic, a former musician in the Sarajevo Opera and Philharmonic Orchestras, who played his cello in public space (in fact directly within "snipers alley") in defiance of the snipers in the hills in order to commemorate some of their victims.[88] While a UN arms embargo had left the residents of Sarajevo virtually defenseless against the well-armed Serb invaders and snipers, Smailovic had a counter-weapon. As he puts it, "I never stopped playing music throughout the siege. My weapon was my cello."[89]

The film director, Ahmed Imamović, takes that cello-as-weapon trope and fashions a story of love and exile that takes place in the midst of the siege of Sarajevo. His film *Go West* (2005) features a Bosnian cellist, Kenan (Mario Drmac) and a Serb military recruit, Milan (Tarik Filipovic), who as clandestine gay lovers, must escape from Sarajevo when the war begins in 1992. Because Kenan is at risk from Serbian militiamen, who check to see if men are Bosnians by pulling down their pants to look for circumcisions, Milan decides to disguise his lover as a woman and bring him to his family enclave, a Serb stronghold in a village in eastern Bosnia (Image 3).

Image 3: Kenan and Milan

Thematically, the film exposes a level of precariousness
that exceeds what results from ethnic antagonisms. Added
to the already complex interstitial identity forces of ethnicity, religion, political history and nationalist aspirations
is a sexual identity that is anathema to the macho male
cultures that cut across the other identity markers. That
identity, if discovered, would imperil not only Kenan and
Milan's relationship but threaten their lives. In terms of
form, the film works through dramatic juxtapositions
rather than dramatic action. It belongs to what Deleuze
famously calls a "cinema of seeing" (in which the viewer
is encouraged to wonder what she/he is seeing rather
than merely what will happen next).[90] The opening scene
in a concert hall locates a segment of the Bosnian life-
world – an upper bourgeois, fashionably dressed, arts-
consuming audience and a genre of performance – that
looks indistinguishable from what one would see in any
western capital. In that part of Bosnia, the West is always
already there in the East rather than being merely a distant
place of refuge. In radical contrast, when the scene shifts
to Milan's ethnic enclave in the mountains, the world

looks distinctively local and rustic. For example, in juxtaposition to Kenan's violin, significant noises issue from the
tree-cutting chain saws of two burly semi-clad twins, who
wave their saws around wherever they go and could not
look more culturally different from those in the Sarajevo
concert hall; they are distinctively local. When Milan goes
off to war, Kenan resides as his wife in the village, managing the impersonation until his secret is discovered by a
woman, Ranka (Mirjana Karanovic), who blackmails him
into sexual relations. After Milan dies in the war, and his
father, Ljubo (Rade Serbedzija) the village patriarch, dis-
covers Kenan's secret, rather than rejecting him or brutal-
izing him, he protects him (a gay Bosnian in the midst of
an exceedingly macho and nationalist Serb stronghold).
He gives him his blessing and some cash, and urges him
to "go west."

The film adds a dimension to the east-west traffic provoked by the war and maintains an affective tension. It
both exposes some of the precarious lives it features and
gives the viewer a palpable sense of the danger that Kenan
and Milan faced as encounters in the village – for example
the boisterous intimacy of Milan's friend, Lunjo (Haris
Burina), and the suspicious lurking of Ranka – continuously threaten to expose the lovers' subterfuge. By situating such an added and imperiled identity issue in the midst
of the already fraught identity/difference perspectives that
fueled the war, the film exposes the tensions between individual and collective identities and the pressures one experiences in attempting to negotiate one's place in a situation
in which all identities are receiving special scrutiny. In such
circumstances, the exposure of a fraudulent (and culturally
abjured) one provides a crucial test. It can invite a violent
or a tolerant and forgiving reaction. In opting for the latter
in the last scenario, the film offers a moment of redemp-
tion. Its title, *Go West*, has a double resonance. On the
one hand, it refers to the reprieve that Milan's father provides for Kenan, helping him to head toward a space with
more tolerance. On the other, it refers to the art of cinema,

to Imamović's turn to an art that developed in the West in order to challenge the oppressive identity matrix (including the taboo subject of homosexuality) that has led to and exacerbated the atrocities in the Balkans. Thus the film genre, like the concert, challenges the very distinction between east and west.

At the very end of the film, Kenan, who begins the film with a documentary-style commentary (in what turns out to be an interview) about fleeing from the hatred that had descended on Bosnia, where "Serbs hate Muslims, Muslims don't like Serbs, Croatian Catholics are ambivalent about Muslims, and they all hate homosexuals," resumes the interview. After enumerating his losses, he states that he still has his music. When the interviewer asks how that can be so when he no longer has his cello, he begins a simulation of playing the cello, which the soundtrack picks up. When the interviewer (played by Jeanne Moreau) apologizes, saying she was unable to hear it, he ends the film by saying he should have played more loudly.

The Balkans War has inspired diverse artistic reactions (other counter-weapons), and among the most notable are the novels and stories of exilic Bosnians. The diasporic flood of Bosnians precipitated by the siege continues to produce a literature that testifies to some of the postwar residual identity experiences that circulate within a global life-world. And while international tribunals have been involved with trying war crimes perpetrators, some of the exilic Bosnian writers have been putting *themselves* as subjects on trial, as their texts think about the implications of the Balkans war. Their work shows in effect how "the act of thinking puts subjectivity into crisis."[91] Here I want to call attention briefly to two exemplary exilic Bosnian novelists.

In his novelistic treatment of the violence in Bosnia, Ismet Prcic composes stark juxtapositions of distant news media views with what was happening "on the ground" as his protagonist and alter ego describes what he sees and hears:

Somewhere behind me the radio murmured about no fly zones, cease-fire agreements, and what Richard Holbrook had said at a press conference about the Srebrenica massacre. And like that, it is a week earlier my mother wakes me and asks me to get dressed…We go outside…I look and see a UN truck pass down Juzna Magistralia and, for a second, cannot fathom what's in it…it's a convoy…Up close we see people, all women, so packed in the back of open trucks that they look like slid, uniform blocks of human meat…We can hear wailing here and there. But mostly they don't wail. They are so compressed that there isn't enough air for breathing and wailing. Just breathing. Barely, What is this? I ask. Refugees from Srebrenica, my mother says.[92]

In his *Shards*, Prcic invents himself as an exile, and to compensate for having left the warscape in Bosnia, he invents an alter ego he names Mustafa who stays to fight. Thus while, as I have emphasized, there are shadow worlds within the familiar the geopolitical world, which complicate macropolitical perspectives, there are also shadows at a micropolitical level. Carl Jung famously insisted that every conscious subject contains an unrecognized shadow subject within, that in effect "we carry our past with us" and "we invariably have to deal with a considerably intensified shadow."[93] Jung's therapeutic suggestion is that the success of psychotherapeutic treatment requires that the subject learn to live with that shadow. Prcic's shadow is an aesthetic counter-subject whose role is articulated in an aesthetic rather than a psychoanalytic idiom. Instead of merely living with it, the subject/author lends it a role that he has escaped. Mustafa is introduced on the novel's first page: "(…an excerpt from *notebook one: the escape* by ismet prcic)":

In wartimes, when his country needed him most – his shooting figure for defending, his body for a shield, his sanity and humanity as a sacrifice for future generations, his blood for fertilization of its soil – in these pressing times, Mustafa's special forces combat training lasted twelve days...He did countless push-ups, chin-ups and squats, lunges and curls, mindless repetitions designed not to make him fit but to break him, so that [he became]...one who was too scared not to follow orders and who would fucking die when he was told to fucking die.[94]

Later in the novel, Prcic, as himself, laments his flight from Bosnia and explains why he needs a Mustafa:

I was never forced to eat human testicles or shoot another human being or watch pigs eat my fellow citizens. No, I ran away instead. That's what I did. That's *my* story. I left my mother behind, my father, my brother, my first love. That's it. The end. That's why Mustafa is here, the shadow under the house...[95]

Like Prcic, another exilic Bosnian writer, Aleksandar Hemon, invents a shadow, an aesthetic subject/character who stands in for him and animates his (absent) experience of the siege of Sarajevo. His shadow, Jozef Pronek, is an exiled writer with a menial job (in a sandwich shop in Chicago, much like Hemon). Serving as a vehicle for Hemon's complex, bi-city identity as he seeks to become at home in Chicago, Pronek observes his new city by walking all over it, while at the same time thinking about the letters he receives from a Sarajevo that is under siege. He reflects on what Sarajevo was about before the inter-(pseudo) ethnic violence occurred and, taking advantage of how fiction can deliver precepts and affects, Hemon recalls the sensations of the city – for example describing an encounter with "sensuous signs."[96]

Sarajevo in the eighties was a beautiful place to be young – I know because I was young then. I remember Linden trees blooming as if they were never to bloom again, producing a smell that I can feel in my nostrils now....I remember the smell of the apartment-building basement where I was making out with my date, the eye of the light switch glaring at us from the darkness...[97]

What this exilic literature implies is that to understand what is disrupted for exiles – to appreciate what has been lost – one has to treat not only macropolitical dynamics of official decision-making and war strategies but also what modes of sensation have characterized the way the life-world was formerly experienced. In a passage about the problem of narrating a life, Hemon addresses that issue of inclusion in a passage that captures the essence of what fiction can do, as he recalls aspects of the minutiae of the everyday sensible world:

> The hard part in writing a narrative of someone's life is choosing from the abundance of details and micro-events... If one elects to include only the important events: births, the details, the lives, the humiliations, the uprisings, the ends and the beginnings, one denies the real substance of life: the ephemera, the nethermoments, much too small to be recorded... But you cannot simply list all the moments when the world tickles your senses, only to seep away between your fingers and eyelashes, leaving you alone to tell the story of your life to an audience interested only in the fireworks of universal experiences, the rollercoaster rides of sympathy and judgment.[98]

Hemon's vehicle for recovering his own life moments, his shadow/aesthetic subject, Pronek, represents his own return to Sarajevo. Through Pronek and the grammatical play with which Pronek is mobilized, Hemon makes himself a witness of his own experience. In *The Question of Bruno*, he gives us a Pronek in the third person at some moments and in others, gives him back his voice – for example at one moment as an I-subject, Pronek narrates his experience of a return to his former city, now devastated from the artillery fire from the hills: "*As the plane was descending, I saw ochre patches. Like scars in the greenness of the mountains... The houses along the runway were bullet-ridden, and as the plane was touching down, I felt as if I were inside of a bullet speeding toward a target.*"[99] Hemon supplies details of how Pronek is fashioned as an aesthetic subject – for example in his *Nowhere Man*, where he refers to him, in one of the stories, as a "hero," whose life is "not particularly exceptional" inasmuch as this "gangly youngster," like most coming-of-age young men, struggles to manage romantic intimacies and vocational aspirations.[100]

Ultimately, the aesthetic subjects created in the ongoing exilic literary world provide a micropolitical justice *dispositif*. Taken as a whole that literary world is a cartography that is being ceaselessly altered as it challenges the justice in the macropolitical world, manifested in tribunals. The imaginative space constituted by war-provoked exilic writers can be construed as a global "heterotopia." It's a space from which (to use Michel Foucault's imagery) one can use one's internal spaces – "the space of our primary perception, the space of our dreams and that of our passions [that] hold within themselves qualities that seem intrinsic" – to reflect on "the space in which we live, which draws us out of ourselves, in which the erosion of our lives, our time and our history occurs, the space that claws and gnaws at us..."[101]

Perspectives on space are also a major aspect of Chapter 2, especially spaces of reprieve from the strictures of militarization and securitization. Along with spatial thinking, the chapter explores ontologies of life and the apparatuses through which forms of life are securitized and/or disqualified, on the one hand, or are articulated through counterperspectives evinced to liberate life from forces of securitization and disqualification, on the other.

2
Atrocity, Securitization, and Exuberant Lines of Flight

"Stuck in this Body"

One encounter in Season 2, episode 13 of the television series *Nip/Tuck* begins with the usual scenario. The plastic surgeons, Sean McNamara and Christian Troy, ask their prospective client (a Latina), "What don't you like about yourself Ms Naves?" The answer they get – "I want to look like J Lo" (the actress Jennifer Lopez) – surprises them. Dr McNamara replies, "May I ask why?" "Because her life is better than mine," she replies. When the doctors seek clarification, asking for example if she wants a larger "backside," she responds, "I already have that, I want to change the rest." When Dr McNamara retorts, "We are not in the business of celebrity look-alike make-overs." Ms Naves makes it clear that she is not simply seeking to make her body an avatar of her idolization of J Lo. The treatment she seeks is essential to the career she wants: "I could have a big career like J Lo – if I looked more like her...I'm not enough...all I get is rejections."

As the conversation continues, it becomes evident that Ms Naves cannot yet pay for all the surgeries she would need (costing somewhere in the neighborhood of $50,000).

She indicates that she expected that it would take such an amount and says, "I'll pay you back when I make it." Dr McNamara responds, "We only take on pro bono work if it's life-threatening." "It *is* life threatening," she asserts, "I mean it's everything I've worked for my entire life...I want to touch people, but the world won't let me because *I'm stuck in this body.*" Although for dramatic purposes the conversation has built-in affective resonance during the give and take between the doctors and their potential client (whom they ultimately reject), it can also be illuminating as a fundamentally political exchange, an instance of the politicization of life.

If we turn to J.-F. Lyotard's philosophy of experience, in which he develops the concept of the "differend," we can see the conversation as a "battle of phrases." In place of Immanuel Kant's figuration of philosophy as a "tribunal," where "critical philosophy is in the position of a juridical authority," Lyotard substitutes the battlefield.[1] Arguing that Kant's model cannot comprehend the negative events that engender "the exploding of language into families of heteronomous language games," Lyotard insists, "we need a philosophy of phrases rather than one of the faculties of the subject."[2] As he puts it in his extended treatment of a philosophy of language, "As distinguished from a litigation, a differend would be the case of conflict between (at least) two parties, that cannot be equitably resolved for lack of a rule of judgment applicable to both arguments. One side's legitimacy does not imply the other's lack of legitimacy."[3]

I have evoked Lyotard's differend here initially at the level of discursive exchange. However, to capture the encounter between Ms Naves and the doctors, it's also necessary to evoke the more fundamentally philosophical Lyotard who famously gives priority to the visual. Ms Naves fumbles for words during the interrogation with the doctors because more is going on than argumentation. The setting contains not only a discursive space but also "another, figural space."[4] The camera shots reveal exchanges of looks as Ms Naves searches the faces of the doctors for approval and assent, while Sean McNamara's face expresses his earnest moralizing tendency ("you're not J-Lo, you're you," he insists) and Christian Troy's face betrays his usual bored self-absorption). Ms Naves' facial expressions and anxious bodily movements express her desire to escape the body she inhabits. Apart from her anticipation of a vocational resource that looking like J Lo will afford is her embodied sense of the J Lo look. Heeding the figural space, we can observe the primacy of an aesthetic sense over her discursive expression of what she wants. Her frequent hesitations during the conversation express the impotency of words, which cannot quite capture the life force that articulates itself in a desire that affixes itself to the look of J Lo, a "figure" that discourse cannot capture. Ms Naves is not merely a speaker; she is a body that yearns, and her yearning is pre-linguistic or embodied as it experiences the object world. Indeed, it is this pre-discursive drive that creates some of the conditions of possibility for plastic surgery. Prior to life as an achievement of social recognition and success is life as desire. What is engaged in a fight of phases is not merely the triumph of one phrase over another but the revelation of communities of sense that must operate without a transcendental basis that can order discursive encounters. In short, although much of the encounter between Ms Naves and the doctors is discursive, they enter the encounter as bodies (they are not merely arguing; they are working in different rooms of the "factory" of desire).[5] There is no unambiguous satisfactory language (as Lyotard insists). Life is also on the agenda in a non-discursive sense, and the argumentation occults a background that speaks to life as aesthetic rather than conceptual, life that at the level of sensation privileges the figure rather than concepts of vocational success.

Nevertheless, apart from the aesthetic, desiring encounter of the bodies in the McNamara-Troy office, the "incommensurability" or "heterogeneity of phrase regimes" that

Lyotard posits as a fundamental basis of social encounter needs to be supplemented, both historically and structurally, if we are to appreciate the political implications of the doctor–client conversation on what is "life threatening" (and thus the political ethos that dictates the responsibilities of medical agency). Such social encounters over the political significance of life operate within a broad ideational terrain in which both public and private agencies struggle for control. For example, pointing to the biopolitical role of governing authorities, Michel Foucault observed that modernity can be politically framed as an epoch of the governmentalization of life, one in which "political power [has] assigned itself the task of administering life."[6] Whereas, "For millennia, man remained what he was for Aristotle: a living animal with the additional capacity for political existence; modern man is an animal whose politics places his existence as a living being in question."[7] However as the *Nip/Tuck* dramas indicate, much of the management of life is now the purview of commercial ventures.

To treat that eventuation in the history of managing life, I turn first to a near future evinced in a Gary Shteyngart novel, which begins with a soliloquy by his protagonist Lenny Abramov, who thinks *his* body can endure forever:

> Today I've made a major decision: *I am never going to die.* Others will die all around me. They will be nullified. The light switch will be turned off. Their lives, their entirety, will be marked by glossy marble headstones bearing false summations ("her star shone brightly," "never to be forgotten," "he liked jazz"), and then these too will be lost in a coastal flood or get hacked to pieces by some genetically modified future-turkey.[8]

Lenny is able to make that "decision" because he is employed "as the Life Lover's Outreach Coordinator (Grade G) of the Post-Human Services division of the Staatling–Wapachung Corporation," a business venture that claims to be on the verge of discovering a technology that will allow them to offer their clients immortality.[9] Lenny describes his position while posted in Italy this way: "I work in the creative economy...indefinite life extension. We're going to help people live forever. I'm looking for European HNWIs – that's High Net Worth Individuals – and they're going to be our clients. We call them 'life lovers'."[10]

Although it is unable ultimately to offer a life extension service ("in the end, nature would not yield," and the corporation eventually gives up life extension and becomes a lifestyle boutique), the appeal of its initial pretention to sell a service to ward off death derives from two aspects of the human condition, one enduring and one contemporary. The former is the ontological depth of life/death, a virtuality that has always hovered over every human aspiration, great and small. For example, French biologist, Xavier Bichat gave the fight against death preeminence: "Life is the totality of those functions which resist death."[11] And nearly two centuries later, Georges Bataille concurred with this quip: "Death is not the only contradiction that enters into the edifice formed by man's activity, but it has a kind of preeminence."[12]

A corporation's search for a clientele for death-related services constitutes an "event," a historic shift in command structures. Corporate capitalism has attenuated the cultural authority of religion's symbolic control over life/death.[13] If we go back historically and look at the motivations engendering the approach to life and death of salvation-oriented religions, we discover a search that is quite different from Lenny's. Instead of a corporate search for "high net worth" clients, there were widespread searches for saints and sorcerers (both allegedly "intimate with the divine") as people sought details on what they could expect from an afterlife.[14]

Anticipating the transition from religion to corporate control over life, Philip Dick invented a historical moment in which corporate control over life/death assimilates a religious motif. In his novel *Do Androids Dream of*

Electric Sheep (and in Ridley Scott's film version of it, *Blade Runner* (1982)), corporate capitalism and religion are inter-articulated. A large private enterprise, the Tyrell Corporation, presides over life and death by making artificial people to help manage a dystopic world. They are "replicants" in the film version and "androids" in the novel version, with built-in termination dates; they are programmed for a four-year life span. The film version's imagery renders the Tyrrell Corporation as a giant temple (in the film's opening shots, the corporation is filmed from the bottom so that it looms cathedral-like over a dystopic life-world). Toward the end of the film narrative, one of its products, Roy Batty, comes to "meet his maker," the corporation head, Eldon Tyrell, saying, in response to Tyrell's question, "What can your maker do for you?" "I want more life, fucker!"[15] Before Batty snuffs out Tyrell's life, gripping his face and pushing his thumbs into his eyes (eye imagery is abundant in the film, doubtless connecting "eyes" with "I"-egos),[16] they engage in a contentious conversation about "more life." In response to Batty's demand, Tyrell asserts that has had "more life" because he has lived his so intensely.

In contrast with Dick's religiously figured capitalism, the corporate control of life/death in Shteyngart's novel functions in a future in which religion has been wholly displaced by capitalism. While the products of the god-like Eldon Tyrell are the people he makes, the Staatling–Wapachung Corporation functions in a futuristic, neoliberal world that has people as their clients, and except for some advanced surveillance practices and technologies, the novel's future world looks a lot like the present. Death-avoiding life extension services are to be available to those who can afford them – subjects that neoliberal economic practices have enabled (the HNWIs that Lenny Abramov has been hired to solicit).

Accordingly, when the Wapachung Corporation shifts to becoming a lifestyle boutique, its life-enhancing services are also available only to a "high net worth" clientele. If we heed the structural context that would supplement the "battle of phases" in the plastic surgeons' office in *Nip/Tuck* over what is "life threatening," economic inequality and differing levels of cultural capital become essential properties. As a result, to appreciate Ms Naves' request for services, we have to understand the transformations in the articulation between the differential levels of economic and cultural capital, resident in social space, that determine "successful" versus "unsuccessful living forms."[17] As visual media have proliferated to assist the shift in economy from production to consumption, so that in the new economic paradigm "commodities themselves were not so much material goods as desired objects,"[18] one's physical appearance has shifted from being a cultural marker, testifying primarily to ethnic membership, to an economic asset. As Pierre Bourdieu famously points out, the dynamics of the "social fields," which alter both cultural and economic capital involved in exchanges in social space, function within a social logic of distinction that effectively enfranchises diverse entrepreneurial service providers (one of his examples of such enabled providers are both new and traditional couturiers who are summoned into a contest for corporate control, cutting clothes for challenging versus traditional elites respectively).[19] What that historical dynamic has done for couturiers, it has done for plastic surgeons, whose services are summoned by changes in the assets required for positioning in romantic, marriage, and job markets (among others).

Doubtless, the pervasiveness of visual media has accelerated the plastic surgery-enabling discontent people have with their body images. Zadie Smith captures that phenomenon in a Belsey family's, mother–daughter exchange in her novel *On Beauty*. The daughter, Zora says, "I need some new shit to wear. I *hate* everything I own." Her mother, Kiki's, response is then narrated thus: "This is why Kiki had dreaded having girls: she knew she wouldn't be able to protect them from self-disgust. To that end she had tried banning television in the early years, and never had a lipstick or a woman's magazine crossed the threshold of the Belsey home to Kiki's knowledge, but these and other precautionary measures had made no difference. It was in the *air* . . . this hatred of women and their bodies . . . "[20] As Smith's character Kiki discerns, the visual media – what's *on* the air – are pervasive and have effectively played into the process through which contemporary "life," constituted as successful versus unsuccessful body types, is a primary political problematic within families as well as in the rest of collective life. The question to which I turn then is *how* (with what conceptual strategies) can we elaborate that politics.

A Methodological Interlude

As is the case in Chapter 1, my approach to life is instructed by Foucault's "choice of method," in which rather than "deducing concrete phenomena from universals, or instead of starting with universals as an obligatory grid of intelligibility for certain concrete practices," he "start[s] with the concrete practices and, as it were, pass[es] these universals through the grid of these practices."[21] As applied here, the method aims not to discern *what* life is but rather, *how* it emerges as a problem, *where* the problem is controlled (i.e., what kinds of apparatuses and discourses are involved), *when* (in what kinds of historical moments) life becomes part of an agenda, and *whose* perspectives on life are in control, or are at least involved in contestation over its interpretation. At a minimum, as Michael Dillon and Julian Reid suggest, "there is no single, simple, or complex truth to tell about life"; and whenever "truth-telling" about life occurs, it presupposes power relations.[22] Moreover, as I have suggested, states are one among various powerful players in the trajectory of historical changes in the control over the warranting of proper lives and the enabling that determines (in Georges Canguilhem's terms) "successful" versus "unsuccessful" human life. For example, although plastic surgery and its practitioners are subject to state regulatory agencies (as well as professional regulatory codes of conduct), a wide variety of extra-state forces shape the morphology-reshaping consumption preferences that summon their services – media-influenced exchanges of recognition among others. And a large number of agencies, both public and private, play roles in creating and policing the boundaries of what are cosmetic versus rehabilitative procedures, where the former are interpreted as the responsibility of the service-seeker, while the later warrant public assistance. Thus the distinctions among the conditions that the plastic surgery clientele seek to alter are pragmatically and politically (rather than essentially) determined by social and legal policing apparatuses. Nevertheless, those apparatuses are responsive to more basic ontological commitments as to what constitutes a proper or normal human life. The relationship between these two levels warrants further attention.

From Ontologies to Apparatuses

Giorgio Agamben has succinctly stated the ontology-apparatus relationship I wish to elaborate and explore in order to pursue a politics of life. In his re-inflection of Foucault's concept of the *dispositif*, he proposes

> nothing less than a general and massive partitioning of beings into two large groups or classes: on the one hand, living beings (or substances), and on the other, apparatuses in which living beings are incessantly captured... [where an "apparatus" is] anything that has in some way the capacity to capture, orient, determine, intercept, model, control, or secure the gestures, behaviors, opinions, or discourses of living beings.[23]

How then does life emerge in the complex spaces between ontologies (commitments to what constitutes a "human" life) and apparatuses (practices that differentially manage human life, for example privileging it against the non-human and the inhuman or prolonging or shortening particular lives)? Historically, diverse agencies and genres have participated in the negotiations that occur between ontological shifts and agency implementations (life disposing apparatuses or *dispositifs*). At the ontological level, the philosophical engagement with "life" has been diverse: versions include "the affective-phenomenological, the bio-political, and the politico-theological."[24]

However to merely list approaches is to fail to heed the tensions involved in interpretive negotiations at the level of ontology. To illustrate those negotiations, I want to consider an exemplary historical moment in philosophical anthropology that Gilbert Simondon has addressed. Noting that for antiquity's Pre-Socratics, the "human soul" was "not considered as different in nature from the animal or the vegetable soul (the significant dividing line was between the living and nonliving),"[25] he credits Socrates with the initiation of "humanism," a shift from an old version of vitalism in which animal, vegetable, and "man" are in the same category, to a dualism, "a doctrine according to which man is a reality that is not comparable whatsoever to any other found in nature"[26] Georges Bataille recycles that dualism in his discussion of Eros, claiming that "work" is the distinguishing characteristic of human as opposed to animal life: "Of course it is work that separated man from his initial animality."[27] And Karl Marx promotes a dualism, based on a similar approach to the separation, but with a Hegelian twist that privileges self-reflective consciousness. Marx's humanism, articulated in his early philosophical work, sees the animal as indistinguishable from what it does: "it *is* its *life-activity*," while the human "makes his life-activity itself the object of his will and of his consciousness."[28] *p. 75 EP mSs*

Whether the discourse is philosophically profound or practical/vocational, if we survey the diverse ways in which the human–animal separation has been thought and managed, it becomes evident that the abyss between human and animal is essential to what Jacques Derrida refers to as the human "autobiography." What is involved, he writes, is "the presentation of self to human life, the auto-biography of the human species, the whole history of the self that man recounts to himself...the thesis of rupture or abyss between those who say 'we men,' 'I, a human,' and what this man among men who say 'we,' what he *calls* the animal or animals."[29]

If Bataille is correct, that autobiography began with a prehistoric scripting, articulated in the narrative drawings on the walls of the Lascaux caves. Reflecting on those narratives, Bataille reads the hunting scenes not as evidence of the fantasies of hungry hunters but as humanity's attempt to achieve separation from animals: "Resolutely, decisively, man wrenched himself out of the animal condition and into 'manhood': that abrupt, most important of transitions left an image of itself blazed upon the rock of this cave."[30] Whatever the origin of the human autobiography may be, my concern here is with how it has been inflected to assert not only separation but also dominance, for among the functions of that autobiography (in which the human is an "*uber*specie,"[31]), is the warranting of atrocity. As Derrida puts it, "No one can deny seriously any more, or for very long, that men do all they can in order to dissimulate this cruelty or to hide it from them-selves; in order to organize on a global scale the forgetting or misunderstanding of this violence, which some would compare to the worst cases of genocide."[32]

It's clear therefore that among what the vitalism-to-humanism historical shift reveals is the extent to which the subject of "human life" emerges from and is constituted by a separation that legitimates radical difference with respect to what kinds of beings can be objects of moral solicitude versus being objects of utilitarian use, domina-tion and/or elimination. In Giorgio Agamben's terms, the diverse "caesurae" between human and animal have a "decisive strategic function in domains as apparently distant as philosophy, theology, politics, and – medicine and biology."[33] Those caesurae have spatial predicates; they're driven by "the anthropological machine of humanism... an ironic apparatus that verifies the absence of a nature proper to *Homo*, holding him suspended between a celestial and a terrestrial nature, between human and animal."[34]

Thus historically, proper human life is always to be understood *against* something else; it requires a *gegenstand*. Without going into an exhaustive genealogy of that against which human life has been historically constituted, certainly theological and philosophical ontologies and their attendant apparatuses of control stand out. After the Socratic institution of a humanism that separated human from animal life was a historical "intervention of the doctrine of spiritual activity, starting with Christianity, but much more still at the interior of Cartesianism [which] constituted a dichotomous opposition... that affirms two distinct natures and not merely two levels, putting on one side an animal reality devoid of reason, perhaps even of consciousness... and on the other side a human reality, capable of self-awareness, capable of moral feelings..."[35]

As is well known, as theologies devolved into coercive ecclesiastical apparatuses, the policing *dispositif* included doctrinal discourses – for example Christianity's dogmatics and apologetics – and agencies and technologies (e.g., printing) for their dissemination (propaganda). The role of print has been pervasive across ontologies, for the relationship between humanism and writing has been crucial in the secular domain as well. As Peter Sloderdjk notes, humanism as a practice aimed at calming the beast within, has seen canonical literatures as a key humanizing practice; it has been "reading the right books" that "calms the inner beast." The "thick letters" from one great thinker to another have provided the "model" that has enabled "the care of man by man," he suggests.[36]

The theological and the secular have shared apparatuses because historically the Christian *dispositif* has incorporated secular policing agencies that have functioned to proscribe various heretical ontologies, theologies and cosmologies and to punish transgressors.[37] At the same time however, Christian theology has occasionally eschewed the more coercive instrumentalities of its ecumenical aspirations in order to contribute to a counter-discourse to the more belligerent historical archives of war that dissimulate human suffering. Some aspects of the Christian global mission, predicated on an articulation of theological and secular anthropologies, seek to install what Paul Ricoeur calls a "culture of *just memory*."[38] With respect to that mission (especially emphasized in the tendency of the Catholic ecumene under Pope John Paul II), theological ontologies and their related apparatuses of implementation have often opposed rather than collaborating with state-run secular agencies.

More recently, scientific breakthroughs in cloning have provoked both religious and secularly expressed anxieties about preserving the normative boundaries of "human life," many of which have been articulated in a variety of genres of popular fiction that have explored cloning. Among these are films (for example Ira Levin's *The Boys from Brazil*, 1976) and novels (for example Kate Wilhelm's *Where Late the Sweet Birds Sang* 1976) that have emphasized the inability of clones to achieve the kind of separation from their heritage that distinguishes the human process of maturation. These diverse genres have raised questions "concerning the kind of life that counts as life, the kind of form that is sufficient or necessary to make one a human, and the forms of individuation that are possible for 'clones'."[39]

A similar contestation over what constitutes authentic and thus protected human life, in this case played out during the George W. Bush Presidency, has surrounded the rise of fertility technologies. Evoking the concept of "the culture of life," Jane Bennett refers to a White House event, a prayer breakfast in May of 2005, in which the president noted his opposition to stem cell research and "reiterated his commitment to the life of human embryos," stating, "We must continue to work for a culture of life where the strong protect the weak, and where we recognize in every human life the image of our Creator." As Bennett points out, shortly after the president (along with some members of Congress present at the prayer breakfast) sought to "work for a culture of life," he was rejecting a "Senate and House Democrats' attempt to tie $100 billion in additional funding for the [Iraq] war to a timetable for the withdrawal of US troops," a war Bush referred to as "vital."[40] In short, "life" as authentic "vitality," has been a significant aspect of national policy struggles (especially since the "life" on behalf of which wars are legitimated has been the defense and survival of the "population" as a whole rather than merely the life of the sovereign).[41]

Legal discourses and apparatuses have also played a significant role in both reflecting on and institutionalizing the separations that have created versions of "human life" and levels of domination and subordination within each version – for example the separation of the "person" as a legal entity, which emerged once a juridically influenced ontology incorporated a distinction between *bios* (mere bodies) and *nomos* (the legal standing of bodies).[42] Moreover, as has been the case with theological ontologies and their attendant *dispositifs*, the juridical contribution to inventing and implementing versions of life has an ambiguous legacy; it has offered protections for some through the historical development of "rights," while at the same time engendering a violence, a "force of law" that imposes subjection and violence.[43] That aspect of the legacy of the law is summed up by Agamben in a remark about justice: "As jurists well know, law is not directed toward the establishment of justice. Nor is it directed toward the establishment of truth. Law is solely directed toward judgment, independent of truth and justice. This is shown beyond doubt by the *force of judgment* that even an unjust sentence carries with it."[44] Accordingly, as Esposito remarks, "Law or right, in its historically constituted form, always belongs to someone, never to all."[45] Ironically, as Esposito goes on to point out, even when aimed at curbing violence, the law has often perpetuated a juridically licensed violence, "a violence against violence for the control of violence."[46]

Turning from the legal to the governmental (Foucault's above-mentioned historical dynamic, the governmentalization of life), the relevant questions become *how* does the modern state invent, differentiate and manage "life," and what are the dominant *gegenstands* through which "life" is articulated through policy? Those questions must inevitably lead to critical thinking about the interface between geo- and biopolitics. Here I want to focus more specifically on two aspects of that interface – biopolitical distinctions and cartographies of grievance – with initial resort to the extreme case, Nationalist Socialist eugenic and territorial violence, initiated when Hitler began purifying and spreading his version of Germanness over the European map. The two forms of violence are articulated in the Nazis' strategies.

In their death sentences for Jews, Gypsies, and the physically impaired, they summoned the territorial model of sovereignty by eradicating their victim's citizenship to cancel their juridical subjectivity, and then they implemented a biopower (in Foucault's sense), not the traditional sovereign's right over life and death, but a state-implemented racism, a biopower that works to "create caesuras within the biological continuum" so that "inferior species" and "abnormal individuals" are identified and/or "eliminated."[47] There was an elaborate biopolitical *dispositif* managing the National Socialist eugenic program, and among its elements was a suborned medical profession in which at least 350 doctors participated in turning doctrine or "ideology into mass murder." "Medical crimes" were perpetrated by doctors who changed their vocation from healers to "biological state officers," working for a state that had been turned into a killing machine.[48] More generally, the Nazi thanotopolitical *dispositif* drew from anthropological (turned into biopolitical) discourses on human life, the most notorious and sinister of which was Alfred Hoche's treatise (noted in Chapter 1), "Life Unworthy of Life."[49]

As its gaze turned outward, the National Socialist State's thanotopolitical and expansionary agendas were fueled by the territorial imaginary immanent in its biopolitical conceits. The Nazis rendered much of the European map as a cartography of historical grievance. For example, Austrians and Czechs became long-term oppressors of the German minorities within their borders. "German life" could not be tolerable in territories of non-German hegemony. As Hitler put it in a 1938 speech in Berlin, focusing on his desire to remove the Sudeten Germans from Czech hegemony, "For twenty years, the Germans of Czechoslovakia have been persecuted by the Czechs... We don't want any Czechs in the Reich...Mr Beneš [the Czech president] must give the Sudeten Germans their freedom..."[50]

In his novelistic gloss on the notorious "protector" of the Czechs, Reinhard Heydrich, Heinrich Himmler's second in command of the SD (Sicherheitdiesnt), an apparatus that incorporated the Gestapo, Kripo, and other parts of the eugenic apparatus, Laurent Binet captures the cartographic imaginary that National Socialist Germany used to legitimate its violent expansion as (among other acts) it carried out Hitler's warning and annexed Bohemia and Moravia to the German Reich and turned Slovakia into a satellite:

Imagine a map of the world, with concentric circles closing in around Germany. This afternoon, November 5, 1937, Hitler reveals his plans to the army high command...The objective of German politics, he reminds them...is to ensure the safety of Germany's racial identity, to guarantee its existence, and to aid its development...For reasons he never bothers to explain, Hitler decrees that the Germans have the right to bigger living space than other races [Doubtless he was in part inspired by Friedrich Ratzel's concept of *Lebensraum*].[51]

"Life" as an Object of Protection and Restoration

There is a degree of biopolitical continuity running from the Nazi's racial purity policies to the present. Although the National Socialist SD was organized almost exclusively around a genocidal agenda, aimed at ridding the planet of biopolution from what were regarded as inferior races, it nevertheless evoked the euphemism of protection (hence Heydrich's title as "The Protector of Czechoslovakia," renamed the "Province of Bohemia and Moravia" while under Nazi control). As Esposito points out, contemporary security apparatuses are also oriented toward "a protective response," often figured, as was the case for National Socialist Germany, within a medical lexicon – to preserve the integrity and wellness of "life" against "someone or something [that] penetrates a body (individual or collective) and alters it."[52] And many security discourses (for example Samuel Huntington's (in)famous gloss on the "clash of civilizations") were effectively Jeremiads about the risk of ethnic pollution.[53] Huntington's protective warnings were not singular. Illegal immigration has been "commonly presented by the media as a potential biological risk to the host country."[54] As Esposito suggests, much of security thinking has been dominated by an immunization agenda, which divides into "two different lexical fields, one legal and political, the other biomedical."[55] However, contemporary securitization involves a different biomedical model than the one driving National Socialist biopolitics. *Their* politics was aimed at creating a "biocracy" that was responsive to a "biomedical ethos," a "positive eugenics," aimed at sustaining "good heredity."[56] The contemporary protective apparatuses are different; they are part of a biopolitics that is "called upon to make ["life"] safe by immunizing it from the dangers of extinction threatening it."[57] What drives the threat? Slavoj Žižek's reflections on the xenophobia that emerged during the breakup of the former Yugoslavia are pertinent. He suggests that the cohesive bond that holds an ethnic community together "implies a shared relationship to a thing," and, more specifically, that "national identification" is "sustained by a relationship to the nation qua Thing," which others cannot adequately grasp: "It appears as what gives plenitude and vivacity to our life."[58] And paradoxically, "our Thing is conceived as something inaccessible to the other and at the same time threatened by him."[59]

Inasmuch as the threat of an Other, who compromises (the fantasy of) a shared ethno-national bond, evokes protectionist demands, Esposito's perspective on security-as-immunization is compelling. However, the notion of protection or immunization from the effects of others who threaten national cohesion needs a supplement to be adequate to the more proactive dimension of the global enmities involved in the politicization of life. For example, the recent history of atrocities in the former Yugoslavia cannot be grasped within a version of securitization as merely a mode of protection. After the breakup of the post-Tito, unified Yugoslavia of Serbs, Slovenes, Croatians, Bosnians, Macedonians, Montenegrins, and Kosovars, its separated entities constituted a set of hostile cartographic imaginaries reminiscent of Hitler's version of earlier twentieth century middle Europe, in which several states were alleged to contain oppressed German minorities. In the case of the former Yugoslavia, the grievances are based on histories of atrocity – for example "shared memories of wartime massacres" which fueled the Croatian drive for independence[60] and Ottoman and Austro-Hungarian violent relations with ethnic Serbs in the age of empires, which has resulted in Serbs seeing themselves as "the *ethnic victims* of alien empires," leading them (with the encouragement of ideological nationalists) to connect contemporary Bosnian Muslims among others to the legacy of their grievances. Thus in the case of the Serbs, their geographic imaginary of the former Yugoslavia is constituted as a cartography of grievance, owed to being "historically squeezed between Austro-Hungary and Ottoman Turkey."[61]

The contested border and frontier areas that separate the newly emerged sovereignties in the territory of the former Yugoslavia contain ideologically implemented apparatuses that effectively displace what were once complicated culturally shared versions of life with narrowed versions, fueled by a "reductive vocabulary" that allocates differential value to the bodies that exist across frontiers.[62] Salman Rushdie, whose novels lament the impoverishment of cultural lives on the Indian continent, addresses that narrowing lyrically:

> The frontier is a wake-up call. At the frontier we can't avoid the truth; the comforting layers of the quotidian, which insulate us against the world's harsher realities, are stripped away, and, wide-eyed in the harsh fluorescent light of the frontier's windowless halls, we see things as they are... Even the freest societies are unfree at the edge... where only right things and people must go in and out. Here at the edge we submit to scrutiny, to inspection and judgment... This is where we must present ourselves as simple, as obvious... 'I'm not anything you need to bother about... I am truly one-dimensional.'[63]

Frontier and border control apparatuses are one part of an ever-expanding, "life" narrowing security *dispositif*, and in his novel *Shalimar the Clown*, Rushdie juxtaposes an exuberant life of cultural sharing – *Kashmiriyat* (which had once obtained in Kashmir) – to the ontologies and apparatuses of a security-oriented, fear-mongering version of life that articulates the geopolitical enmities involved in the struggle for control of Kashmir, yielding violence and coercion, both on "edges" and within states. Accordingly, in the concluding section of this chapter, I consider alternative ways of conceiving the politics of life by staging a critical engagement with that novel, which, like some of his other novels, enacts Rushdie's conceptual and affective line of flight from the atrocity-justifying and implementing forces of securitization.

Shalimar the Clown

Thematically, what is most relevant in Rushdie's novel for purposes of exploring the politics of life is the text's long lament about the way historical grievances and enmities, reacting against Kashmir's cosmopolitan spirit, have resulted in the apparatuses of securitization and violence that have perverted and displaced what was once a lively, inter-culture life-world in which theatrical and culinary arts expressed an exuberance that was wholly excessive to the world of work and the accumulation of wealth. Kashmir's once ritual playfulness, which expressed ways of being in common for people of diverse cultures and religions, is articulated early in the novel at a moment of celebration commemorating a mythical story ("the day on which Ram marched against Ravan to rescue Sita"):

> Today our Muslim village, in the service of our Hindu maharaja, will cook and act in a Mughal – that is to say Muslim – garden...two plays are to be performed...Who tonight are the Hindus? Who are the Muslims? Here in Kashmir, our stories sit happily side-by-side on the same double bill, we eat from the same dishes, we laugh at the same jokes.[64]

Before treating the relevant details of the novel's exploration of alternative ways of constituting life, the one described in that passage and the one created by a violent struggle for the territory, I want to propose some conceptual analytics to "interfere" with its storyline and affective mood. I evoke the concept of interference because I want to conceive my theoretical encounter with the novel as a "philopoesis" (to which I refer in the Introduction). Specifically, as Cesare Casarino has developed the concept, it refers to a "discontinuous and refractive interference between philosophy and literature,"[65] where the "interference" is one between an " 'art of forming, inventing, and fabricating concepts' " (philosophy) and an art constituted as "the production of a 'bloc of sensations...a compound of percepts and affects' " (literature).[66] The interference "a becoming-philosophy of literature,"[67] provides for a treatment that extracts the conceptual power (and thus political thinking) from a work of art whose primary mode of expression consists in blocks of sensation – its affects and percepts.

One aspect of the conceptual practice I want to summon, for purposes of elucidating the politicization of life immanent in the novel's primary thematic, is Georges Bataille's self-described economic "Copernican transformation"[68] in which value derives not from utilitarian calculation, the investing, saving and hoarding associated with what he calls "restricted economy," but from the ritual expenditure of stored biochemical energy (part of what he calls "general economy"), resulting in "wild exuberance,"[69] Bataille theorizes an economic anthropology of value-expressing events or festivals, moments in which "the possibility of life ["beyond utility"] opens up without limit."[70] He conceives such events as expressions of an ontologically oriented rather than utilitarian "economy," which is articulated in moments when human life transgresses or escapes from merely logical or rationalistic orders and is enacted in forms of play that have no particular goal. Such moments are solely the expression of life; they are moments when "life plays and risks itself."[71]

Bataille's model of economy-as-exuberance helps to situate the novel's thematic as a whole. However, to appreciate how the novel functions specifically as a form, I want to invoke two conceptual approaches to its protagonists. First, although Rushdie offers psychological sketches of his main characters, a psychological lexicon would not enable us to make sense of how the novel thinks through the experiences of its characters. Instead of treating the novel's characters as psychological subjects, we can regard them as aesthetic subjects. Here I am drawing on some insights by Leo Bersani and Ulysse Dutoit in their reading of a Godard film, *Contempt* (1963), a film in which a couple becomes estranged as the wife, Camille (Brigitte Bardot), has her feelings for her husband, Paul (Michel Piccoli), turn from love to contempt, they note that Godard's focus is not on "the psychic origins of contempt" but on "its effects on the world." In the context of cinema, that shift in focus is conveyed by "what contempt does to cinematic space...how it affect[s] the visual field within which Godard works, and especially the range and kinds of movement allowed for in that space." Godard's Camille and Paul are best understood as aesthetic rather than as psychological subjects. Their movements and dispositions are less significant in terms of what they reveal about their inner lives than what they tell us about the world in which they are inserted.[72]

Thus, the novel's main protagonists – Max Ophuls (a former US ambassador to India and a subsequent head of US anti-terrorist intelligence operations), Shalimar the Clown a.k.a Noman Sher Noman (Max's bodyguard and chauffer), Noman's wife Boonyi and Max's daughter, Kashmira, are mobilized in a drama that takes place on three continents and spans several decades. The novel maps an emerging global world that is witnessing the way cultural singularities and exuberant inter-cultural encounters are being compromised by agencies of securitization and violence. Although the protagonists are involved in expressions of passion and violence (Boonyi has an affair with Max, and Shalimar murders Max and becomes obsessed with Kashmira), the novel's literary geography, which treats actions across a global network of sovereignties and cultural attachments, conveys much of its political thinking. As is the case with classic European historical novels, in *Shalimar the Clown*, "geography does indeed act upon style,"[73] and the novel's geography imposes narrative strictures: "Each space determines its own kinds of actions, its plot – its genre."[74] Specifically in *Shalimar the Clown* the interaction between territorial struggles and biopolitical versions of nationalism determine how the characters move and interact across a global, geopolitical map.

However, in addition to the novel's mapping of global, geopolitical space is its treatment of a special space internal to Kashmir, "the great Mughal garden of Kashmir, descending in verdant liquid terraces to a shining lake ...The name meant 'abode of joy'."[75] Foucault has addressed himself to this kind of space, referring to it as a heterotopia:

> There are also, probably in every culture, in every civilization, real places – places that do exist and that are formed in the very founding of society – which are something like counter-sites, a kind of effectively enacted utopia in which the real sites, all the other real sites that can be found within the culture, are simultaneously represented, contested, and inverted...Because these places are absolutely different from all the sites that they reflect and speak about, I shall call them, by way of contrast to utopias, heterotopias.[76]

Foucault specifically cites gardens among heterotopias: "perhaps the oldest example of these heterotopias that take the form of contradictory sites is the garden."[77] In the novel, the garden is constituted as a space in the life-world that is characterized by performative exuberance. It is an aspect of life that preceded the encroachment of the violent securitization wrought by the Indian army and other agencies involved in constituting Kashmir as an object within a global security *dispositif*, as the Indian sub continent became a "biometric state,"[78] focused on surveilling and controlling the identities and movements of (ethnicized) bodies, a space in which governance imposed a false clarity in which "life" is rendered as a controlled, unambiguous ethno-national map, and Kashmir is rendered as a space of "emergency" (where "emergency does not so much present an object to be governed as set the very conditions of governability as such").[79] Whereas, what Agamben has designated as a "camp," a space where juridical protections are suspended, making it space within the order of included exclusions, Rushdie's version of the "the great Mughal garden of Kashmir" is the opposite; it's a space of inclusion in the midst of exclusions.[80]

The contention among alternative spaces creates some of the conditions of possibility for the significance of the actions of the novel's characters. However, while the actions of the novel's main protagonists, Max and Shalimar (Max's affair with Shalimar's wife and Shalimar's murder of Max), provide the major genre effect inasmuch as the novel is a revenge crime story among other things, much of how the text provides a politicized view of the contemporary world inheres in a special feature of those characters. They both exhibit a remarkable plasticity; they are caught up in transformative movements that reflect the nature of the changing world they are in.[81] And crucially, their transformations – Max from a Euro-Cosmopolitan to an intelligence and security operative and from an entertaining raconteur to a polemicist and Shalimar from a gentle, creative artist to a violent assassin (as his playful tightrope walking provides the kind of skill he needs to be a successful "terrorist") – reflect the essence of the novelistic genre with which Rushdie is working, a genre that privileges self-reflection and change. As M. M. Bakhtin insists, "The novel is plasticity itself" because "it is a genre that is ever questing, ever examining itself and subjecting its established forms to review."[82] Moreover, that questioning reflects the character of novelists; they are the kind of "authors" who are (as I note in the Preface) open to themselves by seeing themselves as "unconsummated," as subjects who are always becoming, who are, as Bakhtin puts it, "axiologically yet-to-be." That mode of self-recognition articulates itself through how they fashion the "lived lives" of their protagonists as dynamics of accommodation to a complex, changing world.[83]

Clearly Rushdie fashions Max Ophuls' accommodation to a radically changing life-world as a way of reflecting on his own accommodation. Just as the cosmopolitanism of Rushdie's childhood city of Bombay was destroyed by geopolitical events, especially the partition (lamented in many of his novels), Max Ophuls' birth city of Strasbourg, which had hosted a rich German–French cultural mingling (Max himself is a "Frenchman with a German name"),[84] had its inter-cultural existence destroyed by the Nazi occupation. As a result, Rushdie has Max well-prepared to understand what happened to India: "Because he came from Alsace, he hoped he might be able to understand India a little, since the part of the word where he was raised had been defined and redefined for many centuries by shifting frontiers, upheavals and dislocations, fights and returns, conquests and reconquests..."[85]

Crucially, the stories of the individuals in the novel reflect changing life-worlds as a whole, while at the same time providing a contrast of levels of politics. The inter-state rivalries that have compromised and narrowed how life is to be understood (allegiances threatened and protected by forces of securitization) are at the level of macropolitics. They have given rise to state-run apparatuses of control and violence. In contrast, the life changes for the novel's protagonists function at a micropolitical level, where micropolitics is located in reactions to the forces reshaping the life-world's sensoriums: its repartitionings, its changing social issues, its tensions and new factions, and the strategies that diverse social types employ to flourish, survive, or react in the face of procedures and structures of surveillance and control.

Rather than treat all the novel's complexities (its most important aspect is the way its form enacts the identity ambiguity that security agencies are seeking to eliminate), I want to conclude with a focus on the way (aesthetically) Rushdie's novel addresses the functioning of justice at both the macro and micropolitical levels. At the macropolitical level, what the novel describes when it turns to the juridical apparatus imposed on Kashmir is in accord with Walter Benjamin's suggestion that violence is either lawmaking or law-preserving.[86] The economically privileged strata of Kashmir encourage the occupying Indian army and the local governing body to introduce a "President's Rule" by which security personnel are deployed "with unrestricted powers." They operate within an "amended code of criminal procedure," which immunizes "all public servants, soldiers included, against prosecution for deeds performed in the line of duty. Persons who committed the ultimate crime of challenging the territorial integrity of India or in the opinion of the armed forces attempted to disrupt same could be jailed for five years. Interrogation of such suspects would take place behind closed doors and confessions extracted by force during these secret interrogations would be admissible as evidence..."[87]

At the micro level are senses of justice, expressed and enacted sorrow and outrage at the lawmaking and preserving violence in the new legal codes and in their apparatuses of implementation. The enactment of outrage takes the form of Shalimar's revenge for the destruction of Kashmir's life-world (symbolized in part by Max's theft of his wife, Boonyi). Rushdie introduces that modality with reference to other venues where "justice" has been perverse:

> What was justice, the old ladies [joining Olga Volga, Max's housekeeper] chorused, the toothless old ladies from Croatia, Georgia, Uzbekistan, the widows in their dark cassocks swaying in slow unison with Olga Volga the house super naked at their head, grinding her hips, rotating her lumpy white body like a giant peeled potato, there was no justice, the women keened, your husbands died, your children abandoned you, your fathers were murdered, there was no justice none but revenge.[88]

And Max's daughter, Kashmira, wonders, after her father is murdered by Shalimar, "Where were the forces of justice, where was the justice league, why weren't superheroes swooping down out of the sky to bring her father's murderer to justice."[89] Once she seeks to understand Shalimar, she again raises the questions: "What was justice? Was comprehension necessary before judgment could be made and sentence passed?[90]

At one point, Rushdie suggests a frame for such an understanding during Shalimar's murder trial, as his lawyer addresses the jury:

> It's dog eat dog up there in the Himalayas, ladies and gentlemen, the Indian army against the Pakistan-sponsored fanatics, we sent men out to discover the truth and the truth is what they brought home. You want to know this man, my client? The defense will show that his village was destroyed by the Indian army...The dead body of his brother was thrown at his mother's feet...When a man is out of his mind other forces can enter that mind and shape it. They took that avenging spirit and pointed it in the direction they required, not at India, but here, At America, At their real enemy, At us.[91]

However, the enemy as far as Rushdie is concerned is not merely the US or any particular state; it's the policing of movement, both identity mobility and physical travel. It has been against that "enemy" that his oeuvre as a whole has been shaped. He has desired

> not to be defined by anybody else's idea of where a line should be drawn. The crossing of borders, of language, geography, and culture; the examination of the permeable frontier between the world of things and deeds and the world of imagination; the lowering of the intolerable frontiers caged by the world's many different kinds of thought police; these matters have been at the heart of the literary project that was given to me by the circumstances of my life...[92]

Rushdie's protagonists/aesthetic subjects articulate the life problematic with which he is concerned. Their lines of flight from the geopolitical world of violence and securitization in their early lives exploit verticality. Max, as a pilot in his better days (before being corrupted by his vocation as an intelligence and security operative), avoids the lines by sailing above them. And Shalimar, in his better days (as a performer), is also elevated above the fraught geopolitical ground plan as a tightrope walker. In effect, Rushdie delivers his ethico-political orientation toward life with his aesthetic practice, an articulation of the ethical with the aesthetic that resonates well with Foucault's later writings. Foucault's commitment to an "aesthetics of existence" is about extracting the freedom to shape life in the face of a network of constraints, apparatuses of control that quarantine subjectivity within narrow frames and discourage a generosity toward alterity, not only to others but also to the otherness within that always haunts every attempt to impose a unity on the self.[93] The exuberant approach to "life" that Foucault's late philosophico-historical investigations of sexuality privilege through critique is articulated in Rushdie's *Shalimar the Clown*. Rushdie's ethico-political practice is conveyed through the way the world is expressed by the trajectories of movement of his aesthetic subjects.

Ultimately, the novel provides a counter-justice to the official mode of justice constituted as law-making violence and implemented by apparatuses of security. Although the novel's denouement is enacted in a juridical scene (Shalimar's trial), its form is counter-juridical. It juxtaposes literary justice to legal justice, a contrast for which Shoshana Felman (whom I cite earlier) provides the relevant gloss. After posing the question, "What indeed is literary justice, as opposed to legal justice?" she answers, "Literature is a dimension of concrete embodiment and a language of infinitude that in contrast to the language of the law, encapsulates not closure but precisely what in a given legal case refuses to be closed and cannot be closed. It is to this refusal of the trauma to be closed that literature does

justice."[94] Locating the venue of the trial within her observations about the two kinds of justice, she adds (specifically indicating the ways in which justice responds to the
theatricality of the trial), "...the body of the witness is the
ultimate site of memory of individual and collective trauma
[as a result]...trials have become not only memorable
discursive scenes, but dramatically physical theaters of
justice."[95] Thus although Shalimar's individual body is on
trial, it is standing in for a collective, historical debacle.
The justice being meted out in the courtroom drama pales
in comparison with Rushdie's literary justice, his challenge
to the security-oriented closures and atrocities in the Indian
sub continent.

Rushdie's aversion to the closures and atrocities perpetrated by territorial allegiances and the narrowed subjectivity strictures they entail can be extended to a challenge
to what Deleuze and Guattari call "the tyranny of subjective or signifying constellations" or, similarly, to what
Foucault calls "the coercive structures of the signifier."[96]
To effect that extension we have to think not only in terms
of the territorially constituted subject but also in terms of
personhood in general. For that purpose, we can heed once
again the human–animal separation, one among many that
creates the conditions of possibility for atrocity. Esposito,
referring to the "countering force" of Deleuze's concept of
"becoming-animal,"[97] suggests an antidote: "The vindica-
tion of animality as our most intimate nature breaks with
a fundamental interdiction that has ruled over us," with
extensive implications for atrocity-engendering separations in general. As he goes on to suggest,

> The animal – in the human, of the human – means above
> all multiplicity, plurality, assemblage with what surrounds
> us and with what always dwells within us...what matters
> in the becoming animal, even before its relationship with
> the animal, is the becoming of a life that only individuates
> itself by breaking the chains and prohibitions, the barriers
> and boundaries, that the human has etched within it. [98]

Esposito's suggestion about the thought structure of a counter force to atrocity-encouraging separations is conceptually powerful and inspiring. Nevertheless, we live in an age in which technology-assisted militarized gazes are dominating the terrains of identity-difference. In the next chapter, I examine the way that gaze (as Rey Chow observes) is translating the world into a "target."[99]

3

What Does a Weapon See?

In Philip K. Dick's novel *A Scanner Darkly*, the protagonist, Bob Arctor, has himself as an object of surveillance because he leads a double life. In one, as Bob, he is a member of a household of drug users; in another, as Fred, he is an undercover police agent assigned to collect incriminating evidence on the household's drug culture. The household is surveilled with the feed from six holo-scanners planted inside and transmitted to a safe house down the street on the same block. But what is seen though the scanners is not clear to Bob/Fred, who is seeing himself among others:

> What does a scanner see? he asked himself. I mean, really see? Into the head? Down into the heart? Does a passive infrared scanner like they used to use or a cube-type holo-scanner like they use these days, the latest thing, see into me – into us – clearly or darkly? I hope it does, he thought, see clearly, because I can't any longer these days see into myself. I see only murk. Murk outside; murk inside. I hope, for everyone's sake, the scanners do better. Because, he thought, if the scanner sees only darkly, the way I myself do, then we are cursed, cursed again and like we have been

continually, and we'll wind up dead this way, knowing very little and getting that little fragment wrong too.[1]

Like industrial equipment, automobiles, and a wide variety of communication apparatuses, surveillance technology is part of a complex form of agency; it is constituted as "man–machine assemblages." For example, in the case of automobility, the car is a *"machinic complex"*: "constituted through its technical and social interlinkages with other industries, car parts and accessories; petrol refining and distribution; road building and maintenance; hotels, roadside service areas and motels; car sales and repair workshops; suburban house building; retailing and leisure complexes; advertising and marketing; urban design and planning."[2] The human–automobile relationship thus resides in a *dispositif*, an extended network of commercial relations situated in an ideational field of diverse marketing and legitimating discourses that sponsor and normalize those relations.

Similarly, a weapon, aside from its operation as part of the killing operations of a fighting force, is a complex design and commodity that emerges from extensive interactions among political, commercial and knowledge agencies, all involved in the larger (media-propagated) motivations associated with global structures of enmity and national structures of career advancement and prestige. However weapons move in a more contentious world than automobiles: "World weapons might look a lot like world cars on a wall map, but their implications are far different."[3] Aside from their emergence as commodities, the vagaries of mergers and transversal relations among friends and enemies create tensions between their economic and their political and security projects and thus inhibitions with respect to who gets to hold or use them.

Ultimately, at the points of implementation, the use of a weapon energizes a person–weapon assemblage. Certainly what has been modernity's most basic war-related "machinic complex," (or in the words of Deleuze and

Guattari, "machinic-assemblage")[4] is the soldier holding a rifle, an assemblage that has enabled weapons markets as well as a wide variety of agencies. During the long cold war, the US military rehearsed several models but ultimately failed in attempts to acquire a rifle with the reliability of the famed Russian-invented (and since widely distributed) Kalashnikov: "the world's primary firearm,"[5] which, according to Ordell Robbie (Samuel Jackson) in Quentin Tarantino's film *Jackie Brown* (1997)), is "the very best there is when you absolutely, positively got to kill every motherfucker in the room."[6] However, a much larger space than a room houses the targets in war confrontations, and because the war crimes-inhibiting ROEs (rules of engagement) require difficult discriminations among the persons that are to be killed (combatants versus non-combatants), the issue of seeing from a distance becomes paramount. Therefore, rather than elaborating the complex and politically fraught process in which the US armed services selected the (often badly flawed) competitors to the Kalashnikov, I want to focus on the visioning accompaniments to the firing of the guns they did acquire.

Just as in Dick's Scanner story, vision (seeing "clearly or darkly") becomes a vital concern, in on-the-ground battlefield engagements soldiers must rely for their discrimination of appropriate targets on the optical equipment that either accompanies or is built into their weapons. Accordingly, in an episode reported in Evan Wright's ethnography of a US Marine assault force during the second Gulf War, he refers to the Humvee-commanding Sergeant, "Brad Colbert's," "night vision capabilities on his rifle scope," which along with the vision equipment in his vehicle, turn out to be less than adequate because "in the cramped Humvee," it's too difficult to maneuver in a way that will clarify what his driver is seeing on his thermal imaging device. And adding to the problem, "The NVGs" [Night Vision Goggles] Colbert has on "give their wearer a bright gray-green view of the night and offer a limited,

Images 4 and 5: Brad's Scope and what is seen through it

tunnel-vision perspective but no depth perception" (Images 4 and 5).[7]

At a minimum, in the last Iraq War, military seeing in the dark was managed through a weapons technology that saw darkly. However, "seeing" is predicated upon a complex prolepsis, an anticipatory reading produced by a combination of historically created and currently institutionalized practices, agencies, and perspectives that are the conditions of possibility for what is seen. Accordingly (to return to Dick's story), what the scanner sees is unconsummated as a mere eye. Insofar as the images it generates migrate into interpretations, their resulting meanings are a product of the "gaze." In a psychological register, the gaze, as Jacques Lacan famously identified it, is something disruptive to the subject, a sense of being seen (an anonymous gaze from elsewhere) that disrupts the subject's scopic field, undermining her/his confidence in being in control of perceptions or creating a sense of shame because of the associations it evokes.[8]

Lacan tells a story that is behind the emergence of his idea of the gaze, a sense that one is also an object in the scopic field. "I was in my early twenties... and at the time, of course, being a young intellectual, I wanted desperately to get away, see something different, throw myself into something practical.... One day, I was on a small boat with a few people from a family of fishermen.... as we were waiting for the moment to pull in the nets, an individual known as Petit-Jean... pointed out to me something floating on the surface of the waves. It was a small can, a sardine can... It glittered in the sun. And Petit-Jean said to me – You see that can? Do you see it? Well, it doesn't see you."

Affected by that experience, Lacan renders the gaze as "that which performs like a phantom force... In our relation to things, insofar as this relation is constituted by the way of vision, and ordered in the figures of representation, something slips, passes, is transmitted, from stage to stage, and is always to some degree eluded in it – that is what we call the gaze."[9] Thus the man-in-the-loop of the drug surveillance technology, Bob/Fred, as a divided subject (looking and being looked at), is involved in a complex and alienating perceptual practice. More generally, from a Lacanian perspective, the gaze alienates subjects from themselves by causing them to see themselves as objects of the gaze of others, which makes the field of vision traumatic.[10] Within that field, what is experienced is a sense of a returned gaze that does not coincide with the place from which the subject sees.[11] The resulting trauma for the subject is induced by the recognition that it is not an autonomous agent but is rather caught up in a scopic field over which it has little control. That traumatic effect from the disjunctive returned gaze operates in war theaters as well and is effectively in evidence in several moments of Wright's ethnography of the Marine's mission in Iraq.

Before elaborating the implications of the eye versus the gaze within military operations, I want to go back to its implications in Philip Dick's story and add an aspect of the gaze that derives not from Lacan's eye–gaze distinction but from Michel Foucault's rendering of the gaze, which is developed initially in his investigation of the "medical gaze." For Foucault, the medical gaze is not merely the doctor's look. Rather, it locates the patient/subject (the target of the gaze) in an epistemological field, associated with a new form of governance. When the hospital (or "clinic") became a relay of the state's concern with public health, the patient became a source of knowledge to be used not simply as a basis for an individual cure but for managing the health of the population as a whole. Medicine had become "a task for the nation," whereas prior to the development of the teaching hospital, medicine was about an individual healing relationship between doctor and patient. Thus the medical gaze displaced the healer's look.[12] No longer an object of a healing look, the patient had become an object of knowledge to be interpreted within a complex health *dispositif*, which included government bureaucracies, health professions, scientific discourses, apparatuses of data collection and patient management, accounting procedures, and so on.

To adapt Foucault's version of the gaze to the *Scanner Darkly* scenario, we have to translate the gaze from its psychic lexicon to an organizational one. The protagonist Bob/Fred, who is both an object of surveillance and part of its management, is both a historical product and a part of an apparatus. Wearing a scramble suit that continuously alters his appearance while at the station managing his policing role, "Fred...naturally reported on himself. If he did not, his superior (and through him the whole law-enforcement apparatus) would become aware of who Fred was, suit or not."[13] Thus what the scanner sees extends backwards from its eye/lens to the drug enforcement gaze, articulating a complex *dispositif*, which includes a historical trajectory, beginning with the legal codes generated from the time US President Nixon declared a war on drugs through the policing agencies and apparatuses subsequently created (and the peripheral knowledges and professional codes that shape their conduct), all of which are the conditions of possibility for turning seeing into the said, into the identification of infractions and their perpetrators. And as Dick's novel attests, the contemporary policing apparatuses involved in the war on drugs rely less on weapons technologies than on "the logistics of perception" (Paul Virilio's expression, which heralds the shift in war technologies that had occurred by the time the battle front during the Vietnam War had become a cinema location).[14]

Similarly, what has occurred in the evolution of the military's war *dispositif* – its network of decision-making and implementing agencies, along with the discourses and technologies of militarization that sustain them – is that apparatuses of perception are playing a more important role than those that generate firepower. In Virilio's succinct phrase, "eyeshot will then finally get the better of gunshot" (although given the contemporary technologies, both "shots" often come from the same apparatus, e.g., weaponized drones).[15] As has become increasingly clear, a major consequence of that shift toward technologically mediated vision, which yields the derealization of the target, has been a shift in the agency of the authorization of killing. The weapons themselves, with greater or lesser determination by their users and those who command the users, make targeting decisions. For example, as I have noted elsewhere (referring to the episode when the missile firing system on battleship Vincennes shot down an Iranian passenger plane over the Persian Gulf in 1988), the decision to fire a missile was taken by the ship's "Aegis" system, as the radar siting of the plane entered a computer program whose icons did not distinguish an Airbus from an F-14 Tomcat fighter.[16] In terms of the implications for this investigation, the increased perceptual and targeting participation by weapons themselves complicates the issue of determining agency in judgments of war crimes and atrocities. Although much of the war crime/atrocity issue in recent years surrounds airborne weapons, I want to go to the ground first and pick up the story of what weapons see and who or what they target at the point at which the military gaze begins to be directed through armored vehicles: tanks, Humvees and LAVs (Light Armored Vehicles).

Importantly, as I will be noting, the "man-in-the-loop" of weapons-generated perception, on the ground and in an armored vehicle is also one who exists in a fraught perceptual field, which can be understood with resort to Lacan's version of the gaze. In instances in which the field of vision is disrupted, "he" (almost always a he) is frequently affected by the realization that he is an object of a gaze. That disturbance to the visual field is well illustrated in Katherine Bigelow's film *The Hurt Locker* (2008) in which soldiers become disoriented when they sense that (as a harried and ill-at-ease Sergeant J. T. Sanborn (Anthony Mackie) exclaims, "There are lots of eyes on us)." What is crucial with respect to the Sergeant's reaction is not, as Lacan points out, merely the feeling of the scrutiny of another's look. It is the disruption to the visual field such that the subject (soldier) has a sense that he is not the center of a commanding perception. As a result, he becomes anxious about where he is.[17] In such situations, the soldier becomes an equivocal relay of the militarized *dispositif* i.e. one who is (in Lacanian language) less sutured to the lethal tasks and their related implements (weapons) and thus less prone to implementing the targeting directed by the military apparatus. I pick up that issue later in the analysis.

Seeing Darkly from Armored Vehicles

While, as Evan Wright has learned, the seeing of targets in Humvees and LAVs during the US invasion of Iraq was adversely affected by the vehicle's limited maneuverability, there is also a matter of perspective that results from the isolation that a vehicular enclosure entails. The Lebanese novelist, Hanan al-Shaykh captures its implications through her protagonist Asmahan's epiphany when she enters a tank:

> Now I understand why when they're in a tank, soldiers feel they can crush cars and trees in their paths like brambles, because they are disconnected from everything, their own souls and bodies included and what's left is this instrument of steel rolling majestically forward. I feel as if I've entered another world...There is no window where we are, and the feeble light comes from a bulb, or filters through from the small windows in the driver's area.[18]

The experience of the Marines traveling in Humvees, reported in Evan Wright's *Generation Kill*, and that of the tank crew in Samuel Maoz's film *Lebanon* (2009) both resonate well with the perspective of al-Shaykh's protagonist. Turning first to Wright's ethnography, what he adds are details about the enmities and erotics fueling the Marines' gaze. In both the book/ethnography and HBO versions of *Generation Kill*, Sergeant Brad Colbert (Alexander Skarsgard in the HBO drama series version), the main protagonist is involved in an ethical becoming. Although Colbert is a cool, seasoned veteran, eager for combat ("For him, it's a grand personal challenge...Scary isn't it?...I can't wait")[19] and although the advanced technology in his Humvee often creates a mediated view of his potential targets, he is nevertheless affected (or afflicted) by what he sees and ultimately becomes more observant of the rules of engagement than the mission instructions of superiors have encouraged him to be (their primary code is

Image 6: Marine curled up with his rifle

killing to protect fellow troops whenever there is any ambiguity with respect to whom they are seeing). As both the ethnography and HBO drama series indicate, the "seeing" of targets is screened not only through weapons but also through a highly sexualized prolexis; an eroticized male gaze is deployed on both their targets (as the mantra "get some," equating targets with sexual conquests suggests) and on their weapons. For example, one Marine referring to his machine gun in Wright's ethnography says, "I hope I get to use her tonight." Wright adds, "I can picture him caressing the top of his SAW as he sometimes does during tender moment before a firefight."[20] The HBO version enacts that erotic person–gun relationship with an image (Image 6) of a marine sleeping cuddled up with his rifle.

In the ethnographic version, Wright figures the "invasion force" as a "machinic assemblage" in a way that recalls Hana al-Shaykh's remarks about the obtuseness of men in tanks to their environment, "It all has the feel of a monumental industrial enterprise. It will knock down buildings, smash cars and tanks, put holes in people, shred limbs, cut children apart."[21] And he observes the mediated seeing involved in using the armored vehicles' killing power. For example, describing the LAVs, he writes:

Each has a Bushmaster 25 mm rapid-fire canon mounted
in a top turret...They resemble small tank guns and are
operated by a crewman sitting below inside the vehicle,
controlling the weapon with a sort of joystick...the guns
are also linked to forward-looking infrared scopes, which
combine both thermal imaging and light amplification
to easily pick out targets 100 meters distant in the
darkness...[22]

Nevertheless, for all the mediated seeing by the Iraq War's
machinic assemblages, the "man" portions of the "industrial enterprise" that Wright describes bring their own
mediated gazes to the war. One aspect of their gaze could
be best described (borrowing from Herman Melville) as
"the metaphysics of Iraqi hating."[23] The Melvillean analogy
fits especially well, if one recalls Richard Drinnon's evocation of it in his history of the violence on the Western
frontier, in which he chronicles the Euro-American ration-
alizations for the massacres of Native Americans as they
moved westward.[24] The expressions of Iraqi-hating were
abundant among the Marines that Wright accompanied in
their assault during the Iraq War – for example the frequent use of a racist epithet used against African Americans but adapted to Arabs: "dune coons," Antonio Espera's
remark, "Before we crossed into Iraq, I fucking hated
Arabs,"[25] the remark by one of Colbert's buddies after a
"fat man" with a cell phone stepped out of a doorway and
was shot by many of the Marines, "We shredded him...we
fucking redecorated downtown Nasiriyah,"[26] and perhaps
the most callous verbalized image of all, "Tomato man,"
applied to an Iraqi corpse in the road who had been run
over so many times that he looked "like a crate of toma-
toes in the road."[27]

The HBO version provides a compelling visual frame
for comparing the conquest of Iraq with Drinnon's version
of the Euro-American conquest in his *Facing West* because
the continuing shots of the desert landscape help to construct the plot as a reprise of the conquest of America's
western frontier. In this case, the topological orientation is

Image 7: Heading North

one of "facing north," and this early scene of the armored vehicles in a long line heading across the desert (Image 7) evokes the lines of the covered wagons, headed across the American prairie during the process of the Euro-American settlement.

That Wright's *Generation Kill* "takes up the project of discovering who American...Marines are by locating them in the landscapes in which their combat experiences coalesce" is effectively enacted in the HBO version with point of view shots that sweep desertscapes and cities which are...experienced as disorienting and inherently threatening."[28] The camerawork in the HBO version of *Generation Kill* effects a "dual attunement." With close-ups of Marine (and the Evan Wright character's) faces it provides accounts of the "subjective states of characters," while with its sweeps of the Iraqi deserts and towns it shows the way the Marines are situated in the warscape.[29] In effect, the camera movement effects an ethical response to the Marine's Iraq mission, articulated through close-ups and tracking shots as the Marines head North: As Daniel Morgan points out, "Camera movements are in some ways deeply, perhaps inextricably, interwoven with concerns of

ethics – that, as Jean-Luc Godard once put it, tracking
shots are matters of morality."[30]

Thus the ethical perspective (or at least problematic)
that emerges in HBO's *Generation Kill* is delivered with
images. Throughout the episodes, the camerawork is
involved in raising issues about the contrast between
human perception – a weapons-meditated, technologically
aided perception – and cinematic vision. In the filming in
HBO's *Generation Kill*, like that in much of contemporary
cinema, the camera often restores what the perceptions of
the characters tend to evacuate. Nevertheless, the dialogue
among the Marines is also telling, for it is in their conversations that they are making a world that is alien and
enigmatic familiar by filtering it through the cultural genres
with which they have already been accustomed to interpreting the world they (think they) know. In the war that
Generation Kill is exploring, the filtering genre had changed
from those operating in earlier wars. Whereas the Marines
engaging the jungles during the Vietnam war frequently
imagined themselves in a Hollywood film (Michael Herr
reports one of them saying something to the effect, "I don't
like this movie")[31], the Marines in the assault on Iraq's
cities more often saw themselves participating in the virtual
reality of video games (For example, one Marine evoked
the violent urban crime video game, Grand Theft Auto).[32]
And, ironically, many of those games have a "military
technoscientific legacy"[33]

As a result, while the official military gaze is articulated
not only through the optics of weapons but also through
maps (The HBO version of *Generation Kill* "emplaces
Wright's narrative" with two maps, one "large-scale,"
placing Iraq in the geopolitical region of middle eastern
states and the other plotting the invasion route within
Iraq),[34] the individual gazes of the Marines are structured
culturally rather than geopolitically or strategically. As
they screened their experience of the Iraq War through
their consumption of culture genres (popular and otherwise), the Marines effectively displayed the diversity of

mediated ways of seeing that abound in America's socio-cultural life-world. In addition to the virtual video game worlds they brought to their perceptions of the Iraqi land- and ethnoscape, were a variety of musical genres (e.g., country and western and hip hop), super heroes (one of the more hyper violent Marines was called Captain America), religious codes (from versions of Christianity), and Hollywood films, (e.g., *Blackhawk Down* and *The Matrix*). Moreover, although many of the cultural genres were evoked as positive sanction for their battle engage-ments, some were evoked for purposes of critique. For example the Latino, part "Indian," Sergeant Antonio Espera, equated the war with the Euro-American con-quest, referring to the "manifest destiny" ideological legiti-mation,[35] which he reframed with the remark, "America's 'white masters' (engaged in) the genocide of his Indian ancestors."[36] And he derided the Disney film version of the Pocahontas myth's benign version of Anglo-Indian encoun-ter: "What's the story of Pocahontas? White boys come to the new land, deceive a corrupt Indian chief, kill 90 percent of the men and rape all the women. What does Disney do? They make this story, the genocide of my people, into a love story with a singing raccoon."[37]

Accompanying the cultural genre-driven ways of seeing with which the Marines perceived the war was an affective mood, a *jouissance* derived first from their anticipation of continuing the macho acting out of manhood that they brought to their training (and was exercised with each other in their encampment, shown vividly in early scenes in the HBO version in which the assemblage in the tent looked like a chaotic martial arts tournament (Image 8) and second from the already-noted eroticization of the engagement in which killing the "enemy" is equated with sexual conquest.

However, despite the cultural depth of the gaze that was the condition of possibility for much of what the Marines saw, some displayed a degree of plasticity, a susceptibility to being affected and changed by the return of the gaze.

Image 8: A macho contest in the tent

Those who were became less sutured to the man–weapon assemblage and thus to the military apparatus. In particular, Sergeant Brad Colbert, who like the rest of his company began by anticipating the enjoyment of deadly encounter, ultimately became a somewhat changed Marine, one with inhibitions about the targets selected by the military *dispositif* (as Iraqis returned the Marine weapons' mediated looks as well as their more direct looks). Although the relevant concept here is "empathic vision," we must not conceive of such empathy as a wholly subject-centered phenomenon. Empathic vision, as Jill Bennett has conceived it, is a form of heteropathic identification, an encounter-inspired openness to "a mode of existence or experience beyond what is known by the self."[38] If we heed the Lacanian notion of the return of the gaze as the relevant event, the situation that encourages empathy is the trauma through which the subject is constituted as an object in a disorganized scopic field. It should be noted however that structurally created interpretations often serve to obviate the significance of individualized perception. Inasmuch as the "battle spaces" are "messy," even though the laws of war designate moments when non-combatants are to be warned (for example before a building thought to be harboring enemies is to be blown up), the communication of such warnings is often confusing. As a result, the assault forces have leeway to justify attacks on civilians by for example "shifting people between legal designations, turning 'non-combatants' into voluntary 'human shields'."[39]

Seeing While on the Road

To make sense of the genre-effect of HBO's *Generation Kill*, we have to recognize that among other things it's a road movie. While that film genre has been deployed in a wide variety of sub-genres – comedies, westerns, crime noir films, and so on – perhaps the best matches are the films based on the infamous Charles Starkweather/Carol Fugate killing spree as they traveled through Nebraska and Wyoming in 1958: Terrence Malick's *Badlands* (1974), David Lynch's *Wild at Heart* (1990), Quentin Tarantino and Tony Scott's *True Romance* (1993), Dominic Sena's *Kalifornia* (1993), and Oliver Stone's *Natural Born Killers* (1994).

To situate the *Generation Kill* episodes within the road movie genre, I evoke M. M. Bakhtin's concept of the chronotope, which he applies to literature. Identifying the chronotope as a "time-space" that captures the "intrinsic connectedness of temporal and spatial relationships that are critically expressed in literature," Bakhtin characterizes various historical "chronotopes of the road" and refers ultimately to "the chronotope of encounter"[40] where "the spatial and temporal series defining human fates and lives combine with one another in distinctive ways,"[41] among which is the "chance encounter."[42] Bakhtin's chronotope addresses the way a text incorporates history as both an enframing temporal context (where in this case, it is the series of events involved in the second Gulf War) and as the day-to-day process of covering the ground (which in this case must be conquered or controlled so that the Marines can capture Baghdad).

There is yet another genre effect that must be considered to adapt Bakhtin's characterizations to HBO's *Generation Kill*, the distinctiveness of the television series aesthetic, which involves a "format" or "formula" that is repeated in each episode as the characters experience a progression of relationships with each other and face events with which they must cope as a collective.[43] Apart from dramatic deadly confrontations in the weekly episodes is a background of "uneventfulness" typical of television series.[44] Accordingly, while the road is *Generation Kill's* primary trope, as the Marine unit in focus (Sergeant Brad Colbert's Humvee crew) moves northward, it is both their adventures of encounter and the mundane uneventfulness, which characterize the specifics of the narrative that are in view. Certainly the road as terrain is a major protagonist, emphasized in many shots.

If we have to select a road movie that most closely fits the kinds of encounters featured in *Generation Kill*, perhaps the closest is Oliver Stone's *Natural Born Killers*, in which Mickey (Woody Harrelson) and Mallory (Juliet Lewis) go on a killing rampage as "the surface of the screen seethes with a veritable *jouissance* of killing ... "[45] Like *Generation Kill*, The film explores details about the protagonists while providing mere caricatures of their victims. The latter "are extra people – there to be killed."[46] Moreover, in both the film and the television series, those "extra people" become present as a result of the contingencies of encounter. They are those who reside in the particular landscapes of the routes taken by the protagonists. In this respect, images of maps are ominous preludes to some peoples' deaths (Images 9 and 10).

If we heed what is threatening in the landscapes in both texts, we are encouraged to evoke yet another film genre, Alfred Hitchcock's noir-type dramas in which there is frequently something distinctive about the landscape. As it has been summarized, "Hitchcock's camera typically only

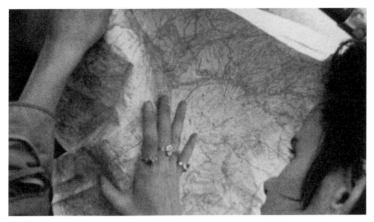

Image 9: Mallory tracing the route

Image 10: The Marines' route in *Generation Kill*

begins by enacting a survey of a seemingly natural scene. Eventually, as the filming proceeds, it becomes evident that there is a perverse element in the landscape" (for example, in his *North by Northwest* (1959) in which a biplane crop duster is fogging the ground where – as a bystander tells Roger Thornhill (Cary Grant) – there are no crops to dust, shortly before the plane attacks Thornhill). Thus, "the film's movement invariably proceeds from landscape to

Image 11: Sergeant Colbert in his Humvee

stain, from overall shot to close-up, and this movement invariably prepares the spectator for the event."[47]

In *Generation Kill* the landscape-as-threat is accentuated in the moments when the viewer sees it from the point of view of the Marines (we see at those moments almost exclusively from the eye-level vantage point of the Marines). And as is the case in *Natural Born Killers*, as the drama unfolds, the viewer also sees the protagonists as threatening. Just as there is tension in the film over whether an encounter will yield another a corpse from an innocent victim, the same tension builds in the HBO series as it becomes clear that the Marines cannot easily distinguish combatants from non-combatants (in some cases) and are not encouraged to make such distinctions (in others). At a minimum, most of the Marines' encounters involve a militarized, weapon-implemented gaze. The series' most typical shot shows Sergeant Colbert, at the window of his Humvee, prepared to see Iraq through the scope of his rifle (Image 11).

This shot of Colbert – often repeated throughout the episodes – is one face close-up among many as the series' already noted "dual attunement – subjective states of the protagonists (face close-ups) and the warscape (tracking and telescopic frames) – proceeds. At the outset of the series, while the Marines are encamped, prior to hitting the road, the close-ups of the faces alternate between the very young, vulnerable, and worried looking types and the grizzled veteran/officers, who appear to be alternatively driven and confused by the upcoming mission, seemingly an image commentary on a line in Wright's book version, which characterized the mission as, "the incompetent, leading the unwilling, to do the unnecessary."[48] And while the book/ethnographic version articulates the different perspectives on the mission by documenting the centrifugal effects of the different voices, which show that there is no single "verbal-ideological center,"[49] the HBO version recreates that plural perspective with close-ups that register the different ways that Marines respond to atrocities, both accidental and intentional.

One frequent face close-up, that of the Evan Wright character (Lee Tergesen), helps to orient the viewer's interpretation of several moments in various episodes, especially those in which atrocities have occurred. At those moments, the Wright character serves as what Gilles Deleuze calls an "attendant," a "constant or point of reference." The "figure" as attendant (which Deleuze observes in the more narrative-oriented paintings of Francis Bacon) can be construed as a "spectator," but not in the ordinary sense. Deleuze's attendant provides the basis for determining the facticity of the scene – in his words, "the relation of the Figure to its isolating place," or "what takes place."[50] What is taking place? Many of the moments when the camera zooms in on Wright's face involve atrocities, in reaction to which he appears troubled (e.g. Image 12).

The problem of distinguishing civilians from combatants is treated in Wright's ethnography as a complex negotiation involving Marines in various ranks, where it seems that the higher the rank the less concern there is with indiscriminate killing. Although the HBO version includes some of the more fraught conversations about the problem, much of the contention is treated with images (especially

Image 12: Wright (on the right) reacting

close-ups of faces). For example, Lance Corporal Harold Trombley (Billy Lush), a Marine sniper exults in killing and is unconcerned about whether a kill is a legitimate target under the rules of engagement. That unconcern shows in his face when he's informed that he has mistakenly killed a young boy.

Because the most threatening moments for the Marines in HBO's *Generation Kill* are represented as they move through cities, the worst atrocities they commit stem from their avoidance of them. As a result, Colbert (in Episode 17) wonders aloud why they have to pass through cities in their vulnerable Humvee, while tanks and LAVs are available for that part of the mission. Relieved when they see a city on their route go up in smoke from the explosives they launch from a distance, they wonder nevertheless whether it's a legitimate target. (Unable to tell if the village had any combatants, they had been instructed from the command behind them to destroy it). And as they close in on an airfield nearby they learn that, "The order is everyone is declared hostile." However, although the most exuberant killer in their patrol, Captain America, shouts, "Engage, engage," Sergeant Colbert demands restraint "We're not engaging; those are civilian huts." And

Image 13: The return of the gaze

crucially, to the extent that Colbert becomes increasingly worried about killing civilians, it is a function of the return of the military gaze by civilians – for example this woman whose son has been mortally wounded (Image 13).

Maoz's *Lebanon*

As I noted, what al-Shaykh's protagonist observes when she enters a tank is also dramatically enacted in the Israeli director, Samuel Maoz's film *Lebanon* (2009). The film features an Israeli tank crew during the first Lebanon War (1982). Almost all of the film's shots are either of the interior of the tank (Image 14) or what can be seen from the tank (Image 15).

However, to appreciate how a tank-target encounter emerges, we have to reach back to occasions that precede battlefield command structures – for example to the acquisition process. Hence, I want to repeat the image from Andrew Niccol's film *Lord of War*, which, as I noted in Chapter 1, captures a telling historical moment. Yuri Orlov (Nicholas Cage) an arms trader who represents the notorious (now imprisoned) Russian arms trader, Viktor Bout, is exploiting the end of the cold war. The East-West ideological divide is past (hence the toppled statue of

Image 14: The interior of the tank

Image 15: The view from the tank

Lenin), and the lineup of idle tanks, whose value Orlov is calculating, are now commodities that will deliver violence on behalf of the highest bidder, provided that the delivery can be consummated, given the illegalities it must finesse (the image of Orlov again – 16).

That the tanks are all pointing in the same oblique direction implies that they no longer represent a specific enmity on the part of the trader, whereas in their first incarnation, they were instruments of the Soviet Union's hegemony within the Warsaw Pact, activated in episodes of repression and atrocity in Hungary in 1956 and Czechoslovakia in 1968. Ironically, in the case of the latter, most of the Soviet tanks that remained in Czechoslovakia until 1991 were

Image 16: Viktor Orlov

built in Slovakia, helping to fuel an industrial expansion that made possible "the livings of tens of thousands of people. From the late forties, Stalin turned Slovakia into a logistical zone dedicated to the supply and equipment of his expanding war machine."[51]

Nevertheless, what makes the tank a desired commodity for militaries is connected with its strategic capabilities. As a result, its evolution corresponds to the changes in logistical modalities that Virilio has described. As a strategic entity, it initially supplied "mobility, protection and firepower," functioning as a primary land component in the period of the industrialization of warfare. Now with infowar and the correlative "digitalization of the battlefield,"[52] the tank, like aircraft and missiles, participates in the derealization of its targets. The battlefield for the contemporary tank is a cinema location in which its "warriors" experience their antagonists in the same way they experienced them when they underwent a simulation training, where their targets were wholly depersonalized and dematerialized virtual enemies seen on computer screens. No longer merely a weaponized "heavy metal object,"[53] the tank's mobile firepower is directed by computer systems inside. As a result, instead of direct looking – even the narrowed version that was supplied when tank crews looked through periscopes (shown in the images in the film *Lebanon*) – its crew has informational and visioning prostheses, and much of the decision-making that leads to the use of the tank's firepower comes not only from deliberations within the tank's interior command structure but also from interpretive agency built into the tank computer's history archive, as well as from remote observers utilizing additional perceptual and informational technologies. The implication for the issue of war crimes and atrocities that such "man–machine" assemblages in the modern tank represents is an ambiguity with respect to the responsibility for the killing of non combatants.

In the contemporary digitialized war environment, which has characterized the post 9/11 wars in Afghanistan and Iraq, in which weapons have gained increased autonomy to make targeting decisions, there exist no effective equivalents of the "joint target list" that the Pentagon created to avoid killing non-combatants; there are no war crimes-avoiding protocols at present to create what P. W. Singer refers to as an " 'ethical' killing machine."[54] Seeking to fill that void, Singer imagines an internal software "checklist" for the rules of engagement built into autonomous robotic weapons that he suggests might ethicize the robots: "Is the target a Soviet made T-80 tank? Identification confirmed. Is the target located in an authorized free-fire zone? Location confirmed, Are there any friendly units within a 200-meter radius? No friendlies detected. Are there any civilians within a 200-meter radius? No civilians detected. Weapons release authorized. No human command authority required."[55]

What's wrong with Singer's "ethical killing machine" fantasy? Immanuel Kant supplied an answer more than two centuries ago. Asking himself about the implications of "man's" direct access to the noumenal realm, specifically to an apodictic set of moral protocols, he surmised that in effect, the human would become a lifeless automaton (read robot!):

The moral worth of actions, on which alone the worth of
the person and even the world depends in the eyes of the
supreme wisdom, would not exist at all. The conduct of
man, so long as his nature remained as it is now, would be
changed into mere mechanism, where as in a puppet show,
everything would gesticulate well but no life would be
found in the figures.[56]

Samuel Maoz's film *Lebanon* (and Evan Wright's ethnography, *Generation Kill*) also supply answers. If we return
to the inside of the tank in Maoz's film, we discover ways
of seeing targets that involve contentious commands and
reactive negotiations among the tank crew and between
the crew and an officer who occasionally joins the them
to organize the mission and impose targeting protocols.
Their protocols, even when followed, are shown to render
their tank anything but an ethical killing machine (partly
because of the "fog of war," partly because of inadequate
training, and partly because some of the commanders
involved have no motivation to discriminate among
targets). As the film drama proceeds, and the dialogue
within the tank develops (while the camera explores the
crew's faces in a way that highlights their anxieties and
lack of confidence in themselves and each other), it becomes
clear that the tank crew is a proletarian workforce with a
high degree of alienation from the commands of its "superiors." They bicker among themselves in response to the
commands of its inexperienced leader, Assi and are more
or less passive in response to the mission commander,
Jamil, who occasionally enters the tank, contentiously out-
lining the mission for the tank crew.

Given the Geneva protocols, the targets should be a
function of the tank as "ethical killing machine." However,
in practice what constitutes ethics is not based on a list of
moral imperatives from which rules of engagement are
derived (to guide either persons or robots). Rather a series
of fraught negotiations within the tank and between the
tank crew and the outer command structure determine
what is shot at, as the crew responds to the threatening

environments that their gaze anticipates (and at the same
time their ability to see is radically compromised by the
technologies of their weapon(s)). No amount of programming can obviate the complexities that interpersonal negotiations and ambiguous technologies of seeing produce. As
I have noted elsewhere, "morality as traditionally understood is about deriving imperatives from fixed moral
codes, while ethical imperatives are invitations to negotiate
meaning and value, given situations of either competing
and incommensurate value commitments and/or alternative perceptions of what is the case."[57] Kant is again helpful
here, for even within his turn to transcendence to mediate
the empirical-noumenal relationship, he eschews definitive
ontological closure for both knowledge and ethics. Ultimately, to the extent that the tank's mission in *Lebanon*
enacts an ethics, it is a result of an act of will in the form
of a resistance of an individual (Shmulik) to commands
that he fire at almost anything he and the rest of the
crew sees.

To appreciate the (ethical) negotiations within the tank
in Maoz's film, we have to heed the complex assemblage
of the crew to which I have already referred. The tank
crew, as an ensemble with significant ethnic and class difference, contrasts significantly with the protagonists in the
pre-industrialized warfare of the nineteenth century. Earlier
war technologies were "manned" by a different social
strata, which was resistant to the devices involved in the
industrialization of warfare: "Ever since the days of Fred-
erick the Great, the military establishments of Europe,
with the temporary exception of France, during the First
Republic, had known a remarkable continuity, with fathers
and sons and grandsons passing through the same regi-
ments, and absorbing the same orthodoxy about the
unchanging nature of war. Even worse, the hierarchical
organization of the army made it into a gerontocracy,
which ruthlessly discriminated against any initiative or
originality from below." And they favored a "conception
of warfare... firmly rooted in the past, in an age when the

musket, bayonet and horse, particularly the latter,]
been the decisive weapons on the battlefield [which they
saw as a space in which the] "individual officer and gentle-
men counted for something." Hence, they resisted the
introduction of the machine gun, for it "represented the
very antithesis of this desperate faith in individual endeavor
and courage."[58]

As is evident in *Lebanon*, the tank's reluctant workforce, engaged in tense discussion about their responsibilities, mirror some of the social and ethnic cleavages in
Israeli society. A microcosm of their social order, their
conversations indicate that they hail from different, non-
professional occupational segments. And while the mission
commander, Jamil, has an Arab Israeli name, the members
of the tank crew all have European ancestry. Their names
– Shmulik, Hertzel, Assi and Yigal – place them as *Ashkena-
zim*. And while the contentious negotiations in the tank
have a significant determining effect on the targeting and
the resulting killing of many civilians, the inexperienced
tank gunner, Shmulik undergoes a dramatic change in
demeanor and outlook during the ongoing assault.
Throughout the film, he is a *becoming subject* affected by
looks that return his targeting look. Ultimately the returned
looks disrupt the field of vision and free him from the
military gaze that his superiors have tried to impose on
him. To put it conceptually, through Shmulik's transformation, rendered in the sequence of close-up shots of his
face and through the returned looks of the war's Others
– Lebanese civilian victims and a captured Syrian soldier,
who is taken as a prisoner into the tank – the film enacts
a contrast between the antagonistic military gaze (and the
looks that the gaze engenders) with "empathic vision,"
where the latter is an ethical concern with victims, which
develops in subjects who undergo perspective-disrupting
encounters and are affected by what they see (I return to
that contrast in this chapter's conclusion).[59]

Thus, although the discourses of enmity that have
accompanied the tank crew's incursion into Lebanon

derealize the singularities of the Lebanese they encounter, it is a series of face-to-face encounters that afflict the raw recruit/tank gunner Shmulik, turning him into a subject whose orientation to the officially engendered antagonism of the conflict becomes radically altered. At the outset of the film, Shmulik is ordered to fire the tank's canon at an on-coming passenger vehicle, a BMW, which turns out to have attackers. Seeing a close-up of the driver on his scope, and having never fired at actual people, he panics, and in the resulting firefight, one of the ground troops is mortally wounded.

As the incursion into a Lebanese town proceeds, Shmulik, seeking to atone for his earlier hesitation, fires on a truck that turns out to be driven by a civilian delivering chickens (the man ends up being mortally wounded with an arm blown off), and he subsequently overcomes his inhibition again and fires his canon into a building, thereby participating in assault force atrocities that maim and kill non-combatants, many of whom are seen as bloodied and partly fragmented corpses. Tellingly, in addition to many close-up shots of Shmulik's horrified expression, when he sees the victims through his scope, are three moments when surviving Lebanese walk up to the tank and return the tank's gaze, looking directly into Shmulik's scope (Images 17, 18 and 19).

Ultimately, Maoz's film enacts an empathic vision by having its primary aesthetic subject, Shmulik pass from perception to action, effecting that mode of vision through its ongoing close-ups of Shmulik by making abundant use of what Gilles Deleuze calls "affection images" (registered in Shmulik's changing facial expressions). In a passage on film images that fits the way Maoz's *Lebanon* manages Shmulik's transformation, Deleuze writes:

> Affection is what occupies the interval [between perception and action], what occupies it without filling it in or filling it up. It surges in the center of indetermination, that is to say in the subject, between a perception, which is troubling

Image 17: Lebanese boy

Image 18: Lebanese man

Image 19: Lebanese woman

in certain respects and a hesitant action. It is a coincidence of subject and object, or the way in which the subject perceives itself, or rather experiences itself, feels itself 'from the inside.'[60]

Thus Shmulik, like *Generation Kill's* Sergeant Brad Colbert, articulates a degree of empathic vision as the former is confronted with the returned looks of Lebanese civilians and the latter with those of Iraqis. However, the vulnerability of on-the-ground soldiers and tank crews to the reciprocity of vision (shown and reflected on in *Generation Kill* and *Lebanon*) is being increasingly obviated as US warfare turns to a far more distancing technology, that manifested in weaponized drones.

Predatory Drones

The drone, which began as a surveillance vehicle and became a weaponized predator, resulted from the commercial and political instincts of two predatory capitalists. As a commodity, the drone was initially a project of Neal and Linden Blue, anti communist aviation enthusiasts, who moved temporally to Nicaragua to assist the "freedom fighters" in their attempt to overthrow the Sandinistas. They liked the drone because, as Neal remarked (while attacking Sandinista pipelines with it), it has "total deniability... You could launch them from behind the *line of sight* (my emphasis)." In 1990 the brothers bought a moribund drone company "Leading Systems, Inc.," that was designing weapons for the Israeli air force. They then started General Atomics (the company that has put thousands into the skies to date). After their first version of the drone, MQ-1, did not fare well in the Balkans (of 68 sent to the air force, 19 were lost) they hired Thomas J. Cassidy Jr., a former Navy admiral to convince his old colleagues to buy them.[61] Fast forward to the present: it's now the case that the Blue brothers' vision constitutes a major part of the military gaze, deployed around the world and most notably in the Pakistan/Afghanistan border region and Yemen, where it sees and then kills alleged "militants" while spreading terror among the local population.

The military gaze articulated through drones works from a great, risk free distance, a result of the contemporary remoteness of military seeing, articulated often through a non professional gaze. As I have noted elsewhere, the "drone pilot" is not always a well-trained

professional soldier with intensive preparation about the
rules of engagement. For example one "pilot" (described
by Peter Singer) was "a nineteen year-old high school
dropout who...was recruited as a drone pilot" because of
his video-game skills, and in another instance, Singer
reports that a "video warrior is helping his children with
their homework at the dining table in a city in Arizona,
shortly after firing lethal weapons at targets in Afghanistan."[62] That "warrior" functions within a complex
weapons *dispositif*, which for purposes of this analysis
involves weapons manufacturers, military agencies extend-
ing from the Whitehouse, Pentagon, and implementing
military services, to the remote warriors who (once given
the signal from equally remote command centers) fire Hell
Fire missiles from weaponized drones. Among what distinguishes the human–weapon assemblage implementing
drone attacks, is the level of mediation that prevents the
"warriors" from being affected by looks back at the military gaze articulated through the drones. Don Winslow
imagines the ultimate *sang froid* of the drone "warrior" in
one of his novels, "some *Warmaster 3* [a video game]
prodigy sitting in a bunker in Nevada knocking back a
Mountain Dew while he smoked some unsuspecting *muj*
[a *Mujahideen*] with a key stroke."[63]

As is well known, as the civilian casualties from drone
attacks rise, so does the level of criticism of the use of
drones in the border regions of Afghanistan and Pakistan
and throughout Yemen, where the planned targets are
"militants" whose insurgent activities, once interpreted,
are marked for assassination (extra-judicial killing) by a
decision-making chain that frequently runs all the way up
to the "Commander–in-Chief" in the White House. In
effect, the ascriptions that constitute "militant" targets
blur the boundary (which historically is always already
"blurred"[64]), between combatants and non-combatants,
while at the same time making the ethics or morality of
war difficult to implement. The ascriptions often come
from a CIA's security-oriented anthropology as the

warrants for killing have turned from "personality" targeting to "signature" targeting (where the latter strikes are
against "men believed to be militants associated with terrorist groups, but whose identities aren't always known").[65]

The cultural "knowledge" articulated by the CIA has
been supported by a suborned social science that has
become part of the military *dispositif*. The designation for
the cultural dimension of war zones is (in military discourse) the "Human Terrain System," and the "system's"
representatives have been recruiting knowledge agents at
meetings of the American Anthropological Association.[66]
Although they have been strongly criticized by that Association, uniformed anthropologists have been embedded in
both combat and intelligence operations.[67] For example,
as Marshall Sahlins points out, "The principal role of
academics in the service of counterinsurgency is to develop
the human intelligence (HUMANINT) that will allow a
triage between those elements of the population to be
attacked (or assassinated) and those it would be better not
to – in brief, sophisticated targeting."[68]

That step toward anonymous killing through a process
in which the killers and those who authorize them (knowledge agents, intelligence agencies, and weapons operators)
are epistemologically, physically, and perceptually remote,
raises obvious ethical questions. Whereas prior to the
advent of such remote killing, "a soldier's right to kill his
or her opponents depend[ed] on the condition of mutual
risk," those "piloting weaponized drones from the other
side of the globe," are engaged in "riskless war," thus
creating a "deep challenge" to what has been called "the
morality of warfare."[69] And in addition to the ambiguity
of what a riskless "warrior" flying a drone from a remote
location can see is the change in the temporal structure of
the targeting decision. The possible interval for sensitivity
to civilian casualties (and mistaken "signatures") has been
radically altered. In the case of drones, "...the sensor
(formerly the UAV [non-weaponized drone]) and the
shooter (formerly a manned airplane, an artillery unit, etc.)

no longer have to be coordinated but are now two-in-one, unmanned combat air vehicles (UCAVs) [that] reduce the sensor-to-shooter gap from hours to minutes or seconds."[70]

Although it could be argued that areal bombing – for example the fire bombing of major populations areas in Japan during the Second World War – gave their pilots a remote view of what they were destroying, the commanding officer organizing the bombing (while participating as a pilot in it) Colonel Curtis LeMay, ordered low altitude flights in order to increase the bombing's accuracy. Many of the pilots were deeply affected by seeing the results of what they did to their targets, even though the victims and survivors among the devastated populations of Japanese cities were unable to return the military gaze that directed the bombing.

Nevertheless, the gaze has been and continues to be returned as various genres of the arts serve as proxies for those who were unable to have their looks back registered at the time. Many feature films – perhaps most notably Alain Resnais *Hiroshima Mon Amour* (1959) – have been such proxies, but here I want to call attention to Errol Morris' *The Fog of War* a documentary that focuses on the career of the former Defense Secretary Robert McNamara, who, when asked about his role in the decisions to fire bomb Japanese cities with dense populations (for example killing over 100,000 with incendiary bombs in one night in Tokyo), responds, "I was part of a mechanism that in a sense recommended it."

McNamara's remark is an exemplary evocation of the war *dispositif* as it was turned to atrocities in the final stages of the war in the Pacific, a *dispositif* that combined strategic and biopolitical presumptions that legitimated the victimization of Japanese civilians. And, as McNamara admits, "LeMay said if we lost the war, we'd all be prosecuted as war criminals." – "and I think he's right." As I have suggested, insofar as the historical victims have been able to return the US's military gaze that was articulated through Colonel LeMay's war plane assaults, it has been

Image 20: Descending numbers and letters

through the proxies of the arts, – for example, films, museum displays, and vast literatures that allow the lives of victims and their associates to rise above the threshold of historical recognition. Morris' rejoinders take the form of a variety of powerful images, showing how a narrow, McNamara-inspired version of rationality was "part of the mechanism that recommended" the atrocities – for example in this image from Morris' *The Fog of War* (Image 20), which substitutes the numbers and letters of calculations for the bombs.

Given the choice of low altitude attacks, the pilots in LeMay's bombing mission were not engaged in riskless warfare; they were vulnerable to anti aircraft batteries. In contrast, the drone "pilots" are not at risk. Far removed from where they send their missiles, they are not positioned to being affected, at least immediately, by the looks of their victims. That most of the victims are innocent civilians is undeniable. The drones "don't see children," said Faisal Shahzad in his guilty plea when tried for trying to "set off a car bomb in Times Square" (as justification for his own targeting of civilians).[71] While the official pronouncements from political, military (and most independent media) sources in the US insist on the accuracy and the minimal "collateral damage" caused by drone strikes in the Pakistan-Afghanistan border region, the best evidence suggests otherwise. The joint Stanford-NYU investigation of the use of drones in Pakistan summarizes the situation as follows:

> In the United States, the dominant narrative about the use in Pakistan is of a surgically precise and effective tool that makes the US safer by enabling "targeted killing" of terrorists with minimal downsides or collateral impacts.[72]

However, as the investigation has disclosed, an alarming level of atrocity has been visited on innocent civilians; "From June 2004 through mid September 2012, available data indicate that drone strikes killed 2,562–3,325 people in Pakistan, of whom 474–881 were civilians, including 176 children."[73] Although there is now a growing political movement in Pakistan protesting the atrocities (as well as a growing journalistic critique in the US)[74] it is too early to find a wealth of artistic proxies for the victims who are unable to look back at the military gaze's UAVs. However, some artists are beginning to provide images of the drone "killing fields" in an attempt to supplant the official reassurances about the collateral-damage-free precision of drone strikes with "empathic vision" – for example with this image (Image 21).

The Empathic Vision of Becoming Subjects and the Arts

To return to the concept of empathic vision I have evoked in the analysis thus far: An episode of empathic vision is a way of seeing that derives from an encounter that yields "an openness to a mode of existence or experience beyond what is known by the self."[76] Two of the protagonists in the texts I have analyzed – Shmulik in the film *Lebanon* and Sergeant Brad Colbert in *Generation Kill* – evince that

Image 21: A drone killing field: *Five Thousand Feet is the Best* by Omer Fast[75]

kind of vision in a way that distinguishes them from others in their combat units. In both cases, they had to be affected enough to extract themselves from the coercive force of the gaze that was directing their units toward their targets. In the case of *Lebanon*, Shmulik's empathic vision is provoked by seeing civilian casualties and the gaze involved in returned looks (he could see them, but they couldn't see him), which leads him to resist his tank commander's orders to keep firing indiscriminately. The effect on Shmulik is shown by his reaction to the presence of a battered Syrian Prisoner, whom his fellow soldiers have abused before shackling him and bringing him into Shmulik's tank. No one but a changed Shmulik heeds the man's requests to let him relieve himself. At the end of the film, we see Shmulik unzipping the man's fly, taking out his penis, and holding a bucket for the man to pee, all-the-while, making eye contact with him (Image 22).

In the case of Colbert, seeing civilian victims of the Marine firepower affects him – for example Iraqi children, such as one who makes "clownish faces" at him. In response to that look, he has his men deliver gifts saying, "Break out the humrats (humanitarian rations); Let's feed

Image 22: Shmulik and the Syrian prisoner

the ankle-biters."[77] And subsequently, he prevents Trombley, one of the Marine snipers, from firing at civilians. As his unit is taking fire from a hamlet and they see heads poking out from behind a palm tree, he says in response to Trombley's request, "Should I light'em up?", "No, not yet, Trombley. Those are civilians."[78] And later, when he sees ("through the scope of his M-4 rifle") a head popping up behind a parapet on the roof of a "little building that looks like a Spanish church," he restrains two of his crew – Person and Trombley: "Don't shoot...Jesus fucking Christ! It's a kid."[79] Toward the end of the ethnography, Wright sees a fatigued Colbert who is appalled by the lack of concern that other units have for civilian casualties. Wright reports, "We draw past a hamlet lit up so heavily by Delta [another patrol]...'That was a civilian target,' Colbert says, 'I saw them'...He sounds tired. I think the war has lost its allure for him."[80] What Wright's ethnography reports is shown with images in the HBO version, as the face shots of the actor portraying Brad Colbert, Alexander Skarsgard, register increasing ambivalence about the war and increasing concern about the deaths of civilians.

Like the two protagonists, the artistic texts I have summoned for the analysis constitute modes of empathic
vision. "Art" as Jill Bennett notes, "makes a particular
contribution to thought, and to politics specifically: how
certain conjunctions of affective and critical operations
might constitute the basis for something we can call
empathic vision."[81] As the arts are increasingly deployed
against the weapons through which the military gaze is
deployed and against what Foucault famously calls the
"truth weapons" that deny the atrocities associated with
their use, they perform a politics of aesthetics by "undoing
the formatting of reality produced by state-controlled
media, by undoing the relations between the visible, the
sayable, and the thinkable."[82] In Chapter 4, I turn again
to artistic texts, this time to pick up and pull the threat I
introduced here in the brief reference to the "war on
drugs," which began during the administration of President Nixon.

4

Borderline Justice

Alex Rivera's *Sleep Dealer*

I begin this chapter with a return to a corporation-dominated future. Recalling the genealogy of control over life treated in Chapter 2, which features two science fiction texts (Gary Shteyngart's novel *Sad True Love Story* and Ridley Scott's film *Blade Runner*) projecting a future of corporate control over life, I turn here to an analysis of Alex Rivera's film *Sleep Dealer* (2008), which imagines a future in which a violent and exploitive border control *dispositif* is managed by a corporation. Rivera's *Sleep Dealer* is a science fiction but nevertheless realistic film (Rivera refers to it as "neo-realist science fiction"[1]) that invents a future of cross-border relationships, "a future that really could be five minutes from now," according to Rivera.[2] The film, set in a future in which the US–Mexico border is totally closed and is patrolled by a corporation's armed guards on the ground and weaponized drones in the air, is prescient inasmuch as there have been continual border control policy demands from members of the US Congress and promises from Republican presidential candidates to build more impermeable barriers and add more surveillance technology on the US–Mexico border (for example Michele Bachman's "pledge to build a double-fencing the entire length of the 2000 mile border with Mexico," and Herman Cain's call for "an electrified border fence, 20 feet high with barbed wire," during the 2011 campaign).[3] And throughout the years of the Obama presidency, there has been continual pressure in the American Congress for stronger security the entire length of the border.

Were such border demands to be implemented, they would extend a border control initiative already in place, The Secure Fence Act of 2006, in which not only more and higher barriers were extended along the border but also new policing collaborations (e.g., ICE, DEA, and CIA agents working with Mexican police) and new technologies of surveillance, including "Unmanned military aircraft [drones]," were effected.[4] In *Sleep Dealer's* future, the border is solidly closed along its entire length, while all the surveillance and weapons aimed at would-be-border crossers (including weaponized drones) belong to a private corporation, located in San Diego. However, the secured border doesn't prevent Mexicans from working in the US. Through a futuristic technology, workers in Tijuana "the world's largest border town" (according to a sign one sees in the road upon entering the city) are fitted with nodes embedded in their flesh, which allow them to be jacked in as virtual workers in the US – as cab drivers, construction workers, and child care nannies (indeed almost every occupational category), while their bodies remain in Tijuana.

A voiceover in the high tech, Fordist-looking factory, where assembly line looking rows of workers are jacked into their virtual jobs (Image 23), announces, "We give the US what they've always wanted, all the work without the workers." US corporate hegemony has created a virtual Bantustan in Tijuana, whose work environment is shown by following one of the protagonists, Memo Cruz (Luis Fernando Pena), who has headed to Tijuana to realize his dream of earning enough money to save his impoverished

Image 23: The virtual Fordist assembly line

family. Before the scenes of Memo in Tijuana, the film opens in his small village of Santa Ana, where he and his family reside, deprived of free access to water because the Del Rio Corporation of San Diego has bought most of the land, has dammed up the nearby river, and charges an increasingly higher price for the water in their reservoir, which is secured by a fence and mounted weapons as well as by armed men who patrol its perimeter. The militarization of the corporation's boundary has turned the Cruz's village into the abstract space of global capital flows, in contrast to the "lived space" of the Cruz family.[5]

The contrast between a powerful corporate America and the Mexican families their enterprise has impoverished is shown through images – for example the towering building housing the Del Rio Corporation versus the squat buildings of the Cruz family enclave (Images 24 and 25)

Briefly, Memo lives his dream of participating in a world beyond his village by hacking into global communications, including the communications of the Del Rio Corporation. Shortly after he and his father go through the degrading process of putting money in a machine at the barrier to the Del Rio Water Company reservoir to obtain water (under the watchful eye of armed surveillance), he says to

Image 24: Del Rio corporate headquarters

Image 25 Casa Cruz

his father, "Why are we still here?" The answer comes back, "Because here we had a future." While Memo dreams of leaving the constricted life-world of his village, his father continues to celebrate what it has meant. Ultimately, Memo's hacking leads to his father's death. When the policing apparatuses within the Del Rio Corporation become aware of Memo's monitoring of their conversations, they track the location and have one of their drone pilots, Rudy Ramirez (Jacob Vargas) lock onto Casa Cruz and blow it up with his weaponized drone (and then fire on the wounded father as he crawls out of his burning home). After that, the grieving and chastened Memo travels to Tijuana.

When Rudy Ramirez, who is represented as a heroic success story in one of the Del Rio Corporation's biographical commercials, learns about the atrocity he has committed, he goes in search of Memo to try and make amends. He is able to find him with the help of Luz Martinez (Leonor Varela), an aspiring writer (and also a "coyotech," who arranges Memo's employment by attaching the nodes he needs for the virtual work). After becoming romantically involved with Memo, Luz, who makes a living by selling her memories on the web, decides to tell his story, and in a world in which connections are increasingly virtual and exploitive, her story touches Ramirez, brings him face-to-face with Memo, and ultimately enables a productive intimacy between them. To compensate for the atrocity of the drone strike on Casa Cruz, Ramirez operates his drone again, this time sending it to blow up the dam in Santa Ana, releasing the water for the use of Memo's home community.

Although Luz's storytelling (which she markets electronically), like the virtual factory in Tijuana, makes use of the virtual space of the web, it nevertheless contrasts with the connection-engendered atrocities visited on the virtual labor force (at one point a worker in Memo's virtual assembly line collapses, and Memo realizes that he too is weakening; his energy is flowing from Tijuana to San Diego, where he is (virtually) helping to construct a building). Rather than exhausting him, Luz's story emancipates Memo. Storytelling (even though it is a commodity in the film), in contrast to the injustice of the virtualization of a labor force, is shown to be an instrument of justice, connecting in a productive alliance those whom a coercive capitalism, using a virtual technology protected by its militarized policing *dispositif*, has been pitting against each other. Such storytelling resists the universalizing discourses of official politics; it "allows us to view [a life-world] as a realm that is linked to neither nation nor race, and is characterized by a plurality of 'incoherent' political actors...that 'produce' innumerable stories...[yielding a] displaced notion of politics...[in] a related web of stories that cannot be subsumed under any higher concept."[6] In the case of Luz, we must add her displacement to that "displaced notion of politics." In exile from her home state, she struggles to adapt to an unfamiliar place. To the extent that one wants to gain a critical view of the politics of identity/difference, as it is brought into relief by the events that move bodies across juridical and sovereign boundaries (in this case virtually rather than physically), displacement is a powerful conceptual resource. Among other things, to be displaced is to be invited into an aesthetic experience, into a reorientation and reframing of one's sensible world. From the point of view of a radical politics, a displacement-engendered aesthetic experience disturbs authoritative distributions of social identity. In Jacques Rancière's apposite terms, "Aesthetic experience has a political effect to the extent that...it disturbs the way in which bodies fit their functions and destinations...It has a multiplication of connections and disconnections that reframe the relation between bodies, the world where they live and the way in which they are 'equipped' for fitting it"[7] With the politically acute, justice-creating effect of aesthetic approaches in mind, I go back to a past in which literature (specifically the novel) is a subject of political reflection.

Policing Atrocities and the Spatio-Temporality of the Novel

I begin this section with an actual border story (which I have discussed elsewhere).[8] The late Mexican writer, Carlos Fuentes, reports a conversation that took place while he and American friends were lost while on a driving trip in the Morelos region of Mexico. Assuming that the regional map had a unitary set of addresses, he asked a local *campesino* the name of the village where they had stopped.

The *campesino's* reply astounded him: "That depends, we call the village Santa Maria in times of peace. We call it Zapata in times of war." In reaction to the surprising answer, Fuentes reflected upon the plurality of temporal presences in the contemporary world: "The old *campesino*" possesses a knowledge that "most people in the West have assiduously ignored since the seventeenth century: that there is more than one time in the world, that there is another time existing alongside, above, underneath the linear calendars of the West."[9] Fuentes then summons his vocation and suggests that the novel occupies a privileged place with respect to illuminating and recovering alternative temporalities. Reflecting on his craft, he proceeds to a consideration of the significance of encounter for the novelist and finds himself asserting that the literary genre is especially attuned to multiplicity, to a plurality of presences, to the multiple spatio-temporal ways of being in the world. The multiplicity to which Fuentes refers was addressed decades earlier by Ernst Block, who began one of his essays with the remark, "not all people exist in the same now."[10] While Block treated the implications of the co-existence of multiple temporalities for dialectical materialism, Fuentes' focus is on writing; literature, according to Fuentes, can bring to presence "our forgotten self [because]...the West, through its literature, internally elaborated a plurality of times in stark contrast to its external, chosen adherence to one time, the future-oriented time of progress...the novel is the literary form that, with most complexity, permits us to reappropriate time."[11]

Examples of Fuentes' insights about the novel's perspicacity with respect to temporal "micropolitics," i.e., assertions of individual sensibilities that actually or potentially challenge macropolitics (the subject-forming codes of formal political institutions within national formations) are legion. For example as I noted in Chapter 2, in his novel *Shalimar the Clown*, Salman Rushdie addresses, through the experiences of his protagonists, the consequences of the frontier and border control apparatuses that are one part of an ever-expanding, life-narrowing security *dispositif*. However, rather than adding examples from the vast literatures that treat the consequences of militarization and securitization in border zones around the globe, I want to continue with Fuentes' observations about nations and temporality as they are articulated in his last reflections on his home state of Mexico. In his novel *Destiny and Desire*, Fuentes' protagonists speak to the contemporary history of Mexico, a trajectory that has led to "Today," in which "the great drama of Mexico is that crime has replaced the state."[12]

As Fuentes surveys Mexico's varying national times, he begins in the nineteenth century, figuring the problem of justice by utilizing the typical way a novel aesthetically figures collective issues by exploring familial ones. His main protagonist, Josué, from a proletarian background, visits his friend Errol's privileged family, who live in a palatial home and exist, as the text puts it, "in the *have* column," while Josué "grew up in a gloomy house on Calle de Berlin." The comparison is then contextualized with reference to Mexico's "nineteenth century": "When the country seemed to settle down after decades of upheaval (although it traded anarchy for dictatorship, perhaps without realizing it), the capital city began to spread beyond the original perimeter of Zocalo-Plateros-Alameda. The "colonias," as the new neighborhoods were called, chose to display mansions in various European styles..."[13] In contrast to Errol's class and territorial patrimony, Josué grew up in a crowed urban scene. Nevertheless, he implies that his class difference does not yield a sense of envy and injustice. He reflects, "Now, how do you quantify familial possession or dispossession? People's opinion of the fair is based on whether they had a good time."[14]

As the novel proceeds, Fuentes implies that the state's governance has been about ensuring popular submission to structures of class privilege by managing the illusion that it governs a "democracy," where more realistically, "The history of Mexico [up to the point where crime replaces the state] is a long process of leaving behind anarchy and dictatorship and reaching a democratic authoritarianism..."[15] And most significantly, as Josué's lawyer friend, Sangines, tells him, "I grew up in a society in which society was protected by official corruption. Today...society is protected by criminals," and he provides an illustration drawn from recent history: "Just yesterday...a highway in the state of Guerrero was blocked by uniformed criminals. Were they fake police? Or simply real police dedicated to crime? What happened on the highway happens everywhere. The drivers of the blocked buses and cars were brutally interrogated and pistol-whipped."[16]

Among the implications of Fuentes' observation that crime has replaced the state is the altered political geography the replacement implies. If we heed Nick Vaughan-Williams' suggestion that rather than fixed demarcations, state borders are a biopolitical process of inclusion and exclusion of modes of life (after Giorgio Agamben's binary, "bare" and thus expendable life versus politically qualified life), the conceptual issue becomes not one of a sovereignty-ordered biopower, as Vaughan-Williams' model suggests, but a biopower that results from the alternative struggle and collaboration between drug cartels and policing agencies.[17] And the allies versus victims scene that the enactments of biopower produces results from the illicit, policing-protected drug trafficking enterprise. That altered mode of biopower is elaborately illustrated through the fate of Laura Guerrero (Stephanie Sigman) in Gerardo Naranjo's feature film *Miss Bala* (2011) (which I analyze later in this chapter). At this point I want to note that Fuentes' literary intervention into Mexico's narcopolitics is not a singular event. It has been largely through popular culture texts, both literary and cinematic, that the complicity of law-enforcement apparatuses with the drug operations in Latin America has been exposed.[18] Although Fuentes was well aware of the extent to which cross-border relations between the US and Mexico have made significant contributions to the displacement of state authority by crime, his focus has been primarily on Mexico's internal dynamics. To refocus the issues, I turn to popular culture texts that expand the policing and crime *dispositifs*.

Popular Culture and the Cross-Border Policing *Dispositif*

To situate the politics of Fuentes' intervention into the narcopolitics of the Mexican state, we have to move north and view aspects of the role of US law enforcement in the "war on drugs." The novelist Don Winslow captures both the relevant historical moment and the diverse policing agents involved in exacerbating the gloomy picture that Fuentes provides. One of his characters, Ben, in his *Kings of Cool* (2012) (one of three novels he has devoted to the US–Mexico encounters involved in the policing of drug trafficking) describes the significant historical moment and thence the emergence of the key law enforcement players: "Nixon declared the War on Drugs in 1973. Thirty-plus years later, billions of dollars, thousands of lives, and the war goes on, and for what? Nothing... Well not nothing ... The antidrug establishment rakes in billions of dollars – DEA, Customs, Border Patrol, ICE, thousands of state and local antidrug units, not to mention prisons."[19] Winslow's novelistic glosses on the war on drugs articulate elements of narrative drama with the genre of the exposé in ways that challenge the official discourses within which the war on drugs, initiated during the Nixon presidency in the 1970s, has been promoted by the anti-drug establishment to which the passage refers.

To provide a brief genealogy of the inter-agency collaborations that have ultimately ended in the law enforcement apparatus that Winslow characterizes, I turn first to a cinematic text that combines documentary and noir genres to disclose the antecedent border policing *dispositif*, which

was located in the US Treasury Department – Anthony
Mann's *T Men* (1947). The film begins with an interview
with a fictional head of the US Treasury Department,
"Elmer Lincoln Hiram," who figures the "Treasury's strike
force against crime" with a series of violent metaphors.
There is first, the "Intelligence Unit" which "cracks
down on tax violators." There is the "Customs Agency"
that regulates incoming products, and there is its related
"Border Patrol" arm that fights the smuggling of narcotics.
There is also a "Secret Service Unit" that both guards the
President and "ferrets out counterfeiters," a "Tax Unit"
devoted to uncovering bootleggers, and finally the "Coast
Guard." As Hiram sums up the collective effect, "These
are the six fingers of the Treasury Department fist. That
fist hits fair but hard" (he notes that sixty four percent of
the federally held prisoners are sent up by these units).

"Fair but hard?" The narrative in Mann's *T Men* implies
that the policing apparatus delivers an impartial justice,
and he replicates that perspective in his later film, *Border
Incident* (1949), in which US and Mexican law enforcement agencies collaborate to end the violence and exploitation perpetrated on border-crossing Mexican agricultural
workers, *braceros*. Nevertheless, *Border Incident*, also
structured with Mann's documentary style, effectively
exposes the conditions of possibility for border violence.
After the voiceover at the outset notes that "there is a vast
army of farm workers…that comes from our neighbor to
the South – from Mexico," the narration turns to a lesson
in the moral economy that accompanies the political
economy of California's agribusinesses, as it distinguishes
the *braceros* who enter the US with legal permits from
those who enter illegally and are therefore exposed to
bandits on both sides of the border: "It is this problem of
injustice and human suffering about which you should
know," says the voiceover.

As the film's pedagogy migrates into its drama, the
action begins with an episode of violence; illegals, captured
by bandits, are robbed and thrown into a bed of quicksand

where they sink to their deaths. The film then cuts to scenes in which policing agents from both the US and Mexico arrive at a meeting for a planned collaboration between US and Mexican policing agents, both to protect the legal border-crossing *braceros* and to prevent the victimization of the illegals. Well into the drama – after the American agent, Jack Bearnes (George Murphy) is killed by the Parkson gang that has been preying on the border-crossers – the film ends with a shootout in which Bearne's Mexican counterpart, Pablo Rodriguez (Ricardo Montalban), is rescued and the Parkinson gang is vanquished. As was the case in Mann's earlier *T Men*, the policing apparatus (in this case a bi-national one) hits "fair but hard." However, the fairness ascribed to the bi-national policing initiative does not extend to Mann's filming style, which privileges a US territorial imaginary. The film begins with an overhead shot of the canal on the border between the two countries and then surveys the rich and dense agricultural farms of California. Insofar as Mexico's value is represented, it is as a rag tag (often comical) collection of human capital, a migrating labor force from a territory that appears solely as a perilous terrain that the *braceros* must navigate. Shown in dark tones, the film's noir-oriented genre – "dark city streets" and "the ink shadows of a western setting" – yields a Mexico that courts death rather than productivity; its soil literally swallows the bandits' victims.[20]

In light of cinema's dominant mid-twentieth century treatment of US–Mexico border exchanges, Orson Welles' *Touch of Evil* (1958) stands out as a political event. It's a cinematic intervention that disrupts the model of historical time (a progressive US and a retrograde Mexico) that had to that point characterized the way popular culture genres represented the ethico-political gulf between the two countries. To summarize the critical effect of the film, In Deleuzian terms it effectively "counter-actualizes" the cross-border experiences interpreted in cinema history by mimicking and then re-inflecting them to "double the actualization [in for example Mann's films and thereby]...to give the truth of the event[s] the only chance of not being confused with the only actualization...[and thus] to liberate [them] for other times."[21]

The radical departure from *Border Incident's* political unconscious is evident in *A Touch of Evil's* opening scene. While Mann's film begins with a "formal framing,"[22] an overhead shot of the canal separating the US and Mexico, followed by a panning shot of US farmlands, thereby "represent[ing] the border as a demarcated boundary"[23] and reaffirming the significance of separated national entities (an agricultural rich US and a nearby labor pool that must cross jurisdictions), Welles' opening is a tracking shot, as a car crosses from Mexico to the US. That sequence ambiguates the border effect, for it "throws up a jumble of vanishing centers."[24] Moreover a noir effect (dark tones throughout the film) in *A Touch of Evil* pervades both sides of the border. Rather than being "fair but hard," Welles' policing agents are morally flawed in ways that render "justice" a result of the vagaries of poorly regulated policing agencies and the contingencies of encounter. Welles' protagonists/aesthetic subjects, especially Vargas (Charlton Heston in makeup that gives him a swarthy look), who, mirroring Welles' decentering of territoriality, is a decentered character. With his two names Miguel and Mike, he is a conflicted body, pulled centrifugally between desire and the law. He is, as Stephen Heath puts it (in his well-known frame-by-frame analysis of the film), "the name of desire" as the Mexican, Miguel, and "the law," as the American, Mike.[25]

Without going into elaborate plot details, I want to note that at a minimum the film's political unconscious, unlike that immanent in Anthony Mann's two police procedurals, arguably shifts the problem of justice from the policing of particular crimes to the injustices of the US's neocolonial relationship with Mexico and more specifically to the violence of law enforcement, as "justice" is implemented in the border region.[26] And most significantly, in contrast with Mann's two border films, Welles' divided characters, who articulate contradictions in both racial and sexual subject positions, fail to resolve conflicts, blur the line between good and evil, and function in a drama that leaves the relationship between law and justice disjunctive and unresolved. Among what Welles' film accomplishes is the exposure of the corruption and crime-complicity of policing agents. On the American side, Hank Quinlan's (Orson Welles) murderous and corrupt actions serve to erase the distinction between law-breaking and law enforcement. And after he has been killed and is found floating in waters between the US and Mexico, his body not only effaces a rigid border separation with respect to crime but also, by mimicking the "wetback" with his corpse, blurs the distinction between the two forms of labor power, the *bracero*, and the police detective.[27] On the Mexican side, although Vargas sees himself as one fighting corruption, he displays more interest in eliminating the corrupt, murderous Quinlan than in the civil rights of the Mexican defendant that Quinlan frames for a crime. Thus both main protagonists expose antagonistic features in both national societies and at the same time reveal the radical separation between the law and justice that Fuentes was to point out years later in his novelistic indictment of the way the Mexican state's militarization of law enforcement has amplified official complicity in criminal violence. However to appreciate more fully the forces that radically separate the law from justice, we have to expand the force diagram well beyond the border area. Don Winslow's novel *The Power of the Dog* and Charles Bowden's *Dreamland* are well suited for that purpose.

The Poesis of Narco-Trafficking

The two writers, the novelist Don Winslow and the journalist Charles Bowden, effectively capture the corrupt and violent practices of the US law enforcement agents involved in the "war on drugs," the former with a novel and the latter with a hybrid text, an ethnography that is punctuated with drawings by Alice Leora Briggs and poetic renderings of the autobiography of the book's main informant. Both have been close to the violence of policing – Winslow as a private investigator, and Bowden as an ethnographer interviewing both victims and perpetrators. They both evince what Foucault famously designates as "fearless speech," *parrhesia*: "a kind of verbal activity where the speaker has a specific relation to truth through frankness, a certain relationship to his own life through danger, a certain type of relation to himself or other people through criticism…"[28] Winslow's novel is an in-depth (literary narrative-oriented) inquiry into the US's "war on drugs." His *The Power of the Dog* links spaces and events whose inter-connections tend to be evaded in official policy discourses. The novel opens in 1975, just after the US's ignominious withdrawal from Vietnam, and its literary geography comprises Washington DC's official corridors, Manhattan's Hell's Kitchen, Tijuana and the deserts of the US's Southwest, the jungles of Latin America, and much of the California-US border. At the same time, the novel maps the changing and fraught tensions between various agencies that constitute the US's justice *dispositif* – the CIA, DEA, and Customs and Immigration Enforcement (as well as some of their Mexican agency counterparts).

Briefly, the novel's protagonist, Art Keller is a former CIA agent who transfers to the DEA and likens his role in the "war on drugs" to his other war experience: "Except for the clothes, Art thinks, it could be Vietnam."[29] And the same subterfuge is in play: "We Americans are just down here as 'advisers'." Here's the scenario, which more or less matches the situation in the historical moment and place, Sinaloa's rising drug trafficking hegemony: "The American war on drugs has opened a front in Mexico. Now ten thousand army troops are pushing through this valley near the town of Badiraguato, assisting squadrons of the

Municipal Judicial Federal Police, better known as the *federales*, and a dozen or so DEA advisers like Art."[30]

The novel's drama mobilizes several protagonists: Keller the DEA advisor, his cynical DEA boss, Tim Taylor, Don Pedro Aviles, the head of the Sinaloa drug cartel, Miguel Angel Barrera, a would-be successor to control over the drug trade (and his nephews Adan and Raul), Sean Callan, a New Yorker from Hell's Kitchen and killer-for-hire who is ambivalently involved with mafia operators, a California woman/courtesan, Nora Hayden, and a Mexican Archbishop Juan Parada. The narrative comprises over 30 years of Mexico's violent drug history, up to the post 9/11 period during which not much has changed, at least in the sense that US and Mexican policing agents are complicit in atrocities while, at the same time, official pronouncements at the level of government in both countries perpetuate what Foucault has called a "truth weapon." As he poses the question, "what is the principle that explains history [and right]?", Foucault's answer is that it is to be found in "as series of brute facts" such as "physical strength, force, energy," in short in "a series of accidents, or at least contingencies." However, governments dissimulate the events of global violence by interpolating the use of raw force into implementations of rationality and right, and in a passage that captures the sense of how the two governments use their truth weapon, he writes of "The rationality of calculations, strategies and ruses; the rationality of technical procedures that are used to perpetuate the victory, to silence...the war...[and he adds that] given that the relationship of dominance works to their advantage, it is certainly not in their [the government's] interest to call any of this into question."[31] The counter to the truth weapon is "critique...the movement by which the subject gives himself the right to question truth on its effects of power and question power on its discourses of truth."[32]

In the case of Winslow's *The Power of the Dog*, some of the critique comes from Winslow's literary geography. The players and forces he sets in motion exist not only in the border zone but also in distant parts of the US and Latin America. Showing that in effect the "border" is "as deep as it is wide," the novel constitutes a challenge to the official "war on drugs" policy discourses that focus on walls and other controls situated on the US–Mexico border.[33] However, the novel's primary critique is constituted by the ways its protagonists/aesthetic subjects are involved less in a war in which narco-traffickers are pitted against law enforcement agents than in a complex set of collaborations in which the alleged "law enforcement" functionaries aid and abet drug trafficking. In particular, the novel points out that in addition to the complicity of the mafia in the flow of drugs, the corrupt Mexican administration along with collaborators in the US intelligence agencies engage in clandestine deals that create the power vacuums that determine the differential levels of success among alternative trafficking operators rather than reducing the flows of drugs through Mexico to their largest clienteles in the US. Moreover, in the novel (as a segment of the history of the cold war attests), some of the trafficking syndicates (the Barreras in the case of the novel, who are fictional representatives of one of the Sinaloa syndicates), manage to get a free pass from the US intelligence agencies by providing weapons for US-aligned counter-insurgency forces in Central America.

In the actual history of Washington-orchestrated covert intelligence and armed violence in the Americas, US anti-drug agencies, with the aim of supporting counter-insurgency operatives in Central America, went further than Winslow's novel suggests. In August of 1996 an investigative report in the *San Jose Mercury News* (a series of articles entitled "Dark Alliance") reported the appearance of cocaine on South Central Los Angeles in the 1980s, a revenue-raising operation undertaken by the Nicaraguan Contras with US intelligence agency assistance. A subsequent book elaboration by the reporter, Gary Webb, exposes the interconnections between American intelligence and the drug sales.[34] Although Webb's investigative report provides very credible evidence of the CIA-Contra collaboration in the drug sales, the CIA exercised *its* "truth weapon." A report resulting from an investigation led by the CIA Inspector General resulted in this frequently issued preface to all of Webb's findings about the connections: "No information has been found to indicate..."[35]

Among the most effective critical response to such official truth weapons is the Charles Bowden / Alice Leora Briggs collaboration, *Dreamland: The Way Out of Juarez*. The text is explicitly aimed at challenging the official truth weapons that promote the effectiveness of the war in drugs. Bowden notes for example that on the Mexican side of the war, "Presidents come and go and pretend to be in charge."[36] And while both the US and Mexico act as if they exercise effective sovereign power and that the war is either under control or being won, he sees through the disguises: "One nation is called the United States, the other Mexico. I find it harder and harder to use these names because they imply order and boundaries, and both are breaking down." The breakdown is such that, as Bowden puts it, he has to "try not to say the names," even as they continuously appear "right there on the maps and road signs."[37] As a result, he suggests that a critical view that can oppose the official truth weapons requires a different cartographic imaginary:

> This is a new geography, one based less on names and places and lines and national boundaries and more on forces and appetites and torrents of people. Some places, parts of Europe, island states here and there, remain temporarily out of play in this new geography. But the Bermudas of the planet are toppling one by one. The waves wash up now into the most ancient squares by the most solemn cathedrals.[38]

Bowden points out that time as well as space must be rethought. The linear model of history as a progressive, justice-achieving dynamic in which lives are improved does not hold. "We try to fit this into our notion of history and for centuries our notion of history has been progressive, that things get better, that an invisible hand guides us or invisible gods guide us, every generation lives better than the one before."[39] How can one entertain such a model in the face of the proliferation of "little houses" where people are tortured and killed, he wonders.

Given the complicity of policing apparatuses in drug trafficking and murder, as illegal businesses employ police and federal agents, Bowden finds the discourses of crime and justice equally anachronistic: "I must find a new language, one that avoids the empty words like justice and crime and punishment and problems and solutions...I can still say this side and that side. I can still say police and criminals. But the words are emptying out and the meaning is flowing down the *calles* and into the sewers."[40] "This war I speak of cannot be understood with normal political language."[41] Aside from the critical approach to language that Bowden provides in the face of the violence of policing, are his specifics. For example one US policing agency, ICE (Immigration and Customs Enforcement) turns out to be especially callous: "Between August 5 and January 14 twelve men were tortured, strangled, and buried at the quiet house, and ICE, a component of the new Department of Homeland Security, knew about the killings and did nothing...officially it was a sidebar detail in an investigation of the illegal smuggling of cigarettes...or a detail in an effort to penetrate the cartel. Or it was all about nothing."[42]

Doubtless the most shocking specifics that Bowden delivers derive from his interviews with "Lalo," a former Mexican "cop" who had aspired to work for the CIA but chose instead to work as an assassin for two of the Mexican cartels when he hadn't achieved his original ambition. However Lalo also worked for both the DEA and ICE as well, agencies that protected him from US prosecution for the crimes associated with his cartel services. The shock effect of Lalo's self-described resume is amplified by the way Bowden's text is partitioned; it's a pastiche of genres.

First, the text is set up with breaks captioned as "Lalo's Song." Bowden suggests that Lalo's words capture the grisly reality of the crime/policing collaborations in violence: "His words catch the music of a new world that is being born."[43] In his first substantial song, Lalo reports on his drug trafficking work after resigning from the Federal highway police, moving cocaine with the help of a corrupt customs inspection agent and learning about the "executions" to settle drug trafficking accounts.[44] Thereafter, most of his "songs" describe executions, many of which he arranged and carried out. Second, the text is also partitioned with drawings by Alice Leora Briggs, which interrupt the flow of the text with disjunctive images that juxtapose mundane, everyday life scenes with death imagery. Thus stylistically, the text's montage effect introduces bizarre equivalences that shock the reader, turning her/his attention away from the simplicity of the objects treated and toward their contexts, thereby providing a sense of the bizarre realities hiding behind the official truth weapons of the war on drugs. In such an aesthetic of shock, "the object character of the artwork recedes entirely, and thus a radical diversion from what attracts…has been effectively achieved."[45]

Ultimately, as Bowden points out in the above-quoted passage about the new global geography of forces that eclipse the old world of geopolitical names, the violent world that his investigation and textual work reveal, is but one neighborhood in a world in which official policies amplify the problems they purport to solve. After pointing out how NAFTA destroyed the old agricultural base of Mexico and thereby accelerated the drug trafficking enterprises, and how the "narc budget" increases in the US has been accompanied by increases in drug use in the US, accomplishing only a vast increase in the prison population, he writes, "the only flaw in my notion is this: the Mexican war is simply part of a global breakdown, the shredding of traditional cultures by the machinery of trade"[46]

Bowden's critique of the official policies is replicated and cinematically enhanced in Gerardo Naranjo's film *Miss Bala*, based on a recent historical event, the arrest of the beauty queen, Miss Sinaloa (Laura Zuniga), who was discovered in a car with members of the Sinaloa drug cartel, along with a large cache of weapons and money in 2008. (Specifically, "she was riding in one of two trucks, in which soldiers found a large stash of weapons, including two AR-15 assault rifles, 38 specials, 9 mm handguns, nine magazines, 633 cartridges and $US53,000).[47] Whether Miss Sinaloa was a collaborator or merely a victim remains unclear. Naranjo shifts the venue from Sinaloa to Baja California and casts Miss Bala (Stephanie Sigman) as a victim whose misadventure unveils the cross border network of narco-trafficking, weapons transfers and policing collaborations that constitute the contemporary drug crime/justice *dispositif*.

"Nothing is Fair"

The remark, "nothing is fair," is uttered by the organizer of the Baja California beauty contest, Luisa Janes (Leonor Vitorica). Although it's a response to Laura's remark, "It isn't fair," when she misses a rehearsal and is removed as a contestant (because she had to escape from a dance hall that had been invaded by a drug gang that killed many of the revelers), the remark has larger significance; it applies to the US–Mexico war on drugs as a whole. The contemporary policy approach in that "war," is the "Merida Initiative," a "partnership among the governments of the United States, Mexico, and the countries of Central America to confront the violent transnational gangs and organized crime syndicates" (since broadened to include the countries of the Caribbean), launched in 2007.[48] Despite the optimistic language of official policy discourse – e.g., "We have agreed with the Government of Mexico to work together in several of the most affected Mexican communities, including Ciudad Juraez," and "...we are moving away from big ticket equipment and into an engagement that reinforces progress by further institutionalizing Mexican capacity to sustain adherence to the rule of law and respect for human rights"[49] – the death rate continues to escalate in Juarez (AKA "Murder City) and the so-called security forces, as Bowden has pointed out, are among the major violators of "human rights."[50]

Like Bowden's investigatory texts, Naranjo's film evinces a critique that effectively challenges the "truth weapons" of official policy discourse. With his primary aesthetic subject, Laura Guerrero, he opposes the macropolitical frame that articulates the big lies of reasons of state and nation-to-nation initiatives of policy solidarity and cooperation with a micropolitical gloss in which a victim reveals how and where "policy" is experienced. Although actual historical events constitute the referents for much of what transpires in the film, their historical sequence is not followed. Although as I noted, Fuentes has argued that the novel is the ideal genre for reappropriating time in order to create a critical perspective, cinema is even more enabling with respect to a critical temporality. As I put it elsewhere, referring to "cinematic time": film is a "genre that is ideally suited to an 'epistemology of contingency'"...because... "cinema actualizes a contingent mode of time; through its 'yoking together of non-contiguous spaces with parallel editing'...cinema effects the 'disfiguration of continuous time.'"[51]

In the case of *Miss Bala*, As Naranjo states:

> We wanted to talk about the smuggling of weapons into Mexico, the death of a DEA agent [at the hands of] drug dealers and the beauty queen phenomenon...Many of the stories were real but they didn't happen in that [particular] sequence of events. The license we took was to create a story where they could co-exist.[52]

The "license" to which Naranjo refers is constitutive of the contemporary cinematic aesthetic in which the "time image" dominates. Distinguishing that aesthetic, Deleuze famously (I repeat quotations from Chapter 1) opposes a "cinema of seeing" to a "cinema of action": In a cinema of seeing rather than of dramatic action, "the viewer's problem becomes 'What is there to see in the image?' (and not now) 'What are we going to see in the next image?')."[53] However, although *Miss Bala* is a cinema of seeing rather than of action, the viewer trying to make sense of what she/he sees is put into the same situation as Laura. The way the film is shot – with rapidly moving scenes and frequent cuts and juxtapositions – renders Laura's and the viewer's seeing unclear. And, as Julia Peres Guimarães points out:

> One of the constant features of *Miss Bala* is a pervasive feeling of tension that muddles the spectator's sense of time. Even though scenes unfold chronologically, day and night clearly identified – the story takes place in no more than a couple of days – the lack of clear dialogues, the subdued lighting and sound effects a sense of discomfort (muffled car sounds, shooting, engines running, etc.) the audience never has a clear sense of what is happening to Laura.[54]

Neither Laura nor the viewers can anticipate what will happen next. The viewer experiences Laura's terror but is often not shown what is frightening. Naranjo: "I think the tension is built mostly in the viewer's mind. It was very important for us to not show the horrors but to put them in your head so you would recreate them... The horror and the crime is something you don't see but you imagine."[55] As Naranjo's statement suggests, much of the film's effect results from the two kinds of space it incorporates. Whereas a novel registers the forces on its subjects with the reach of its literary geography (for example Winslow's mapping of the war on drugs in his *The Power of the Dog*), a film works with images and registers its effects by showing how what is within the frame and can be seen is often affected by what is unseen, exiting outside the

Image 26 Laura being taped

frame. Noël Burch has put in this way, "To understand cinematic space, it may prove useful to consider it as in fact consisting of *two different kinds of space:* that included within the frame and that outside the frame. For our purposes, screen space can be defined very simply as including everything perceived on the screen by the eye."[56]

In the case of *Miss Bala*, one kind of off screen space is often brought into play when Laura leaves a room while the camera remains momentarily behind; it is, as Burch puts it, a space in which "a character reaches it by going out a door, going around a street corner, disappearing behind a pillar or behind another person, or performing some similar act. The outer limit of this...segment of space is just beyond the horizon."[57] However, although many of the interactions of the two spaces are evoked by Laura's entries and exits from the frame, her cinematic Odyssey as a whole registers the larger geopolitical space within which the "war on drugs" is occurring. For example while she is crouched, hiding in the shower of the night club as it is being invaded by the drug gang, we can hear one of the gang members say, "find the American." And when the gang loses its cache of ammunition, we hear a voice saying, "contact the Americans" (ultimately Laura is forced to travel to the US with money taped to her body, to bring back the ammunition; see Image 26). A variety of signs expands the off screen space to a "bi-national entanglement...the license plates are from California, the currency in dollars, the guns imported from across the border, and the principal drug market is the United States. [even as] The carnage...remains in Mexico."[58] Thus many of Naranjo's images of the places within the frame "open up a dimension wider than the 'plot'..."[59]

While Laura's spatial Odyssey implicates the macropolitical, bi-national connections involved in the narco-trafficking and the reactive drug war response, it is the suborned comportment of her body that registers the micropolitics of both (their coercive and violent effects on the everyday mundane lives of those who live in affected areas). The film opens in Laura's small, cramped house, which she shares with her younger brother and father. In that opening, where there is not enough light for the audience to see her face clearly, in the few moments where it might be possible, Laura is filmed mostly from the back, a cinematic statement to the effect that in her dreary, impoverished life, she has not yet risen above the threshold of special recognition. From behind her, we see her getting dressed for the first of many times. As it turns out, this is the *only* time that her dressing (or undressing) is voluntary.

Once she leaves the house, she is headed with her friend Suzu (Lakshmi Picazo) to enter the state of Baja California's beauty pageant (despite her father's prophetic warning that it's a dangerous environment to enter). When she signs up and takes her place among the other contestants, there is a panning shot of the assembled hopefuls. What the viewer sees is a diorama of nervous and forlorn young women, seeking an exit from their deprived and unhappy lives. Before she gets in that line, the abrupt unfriendly organizer, Luisa (Leonor Vitorica), tells her she must get dressed in her contestant outfit. That gesture of control over Laura's bodily movements is merely the first of many such moments. Another immediately ensues as Laura and the rest of the contestants have to walk along a line drawn on the floor. Shortly thereafter, they're told to smile and utter a particular phrase, e.g. "My name is Laura Guerrero and my dream is to represent the beautiful women of my state (here we get the first full frontal shot of Laura, who hopes to exit from the dreary life in which she is seen primarily from the back in a darkened hovel of a house). That enforced remark, added to others that the contestants must make during the final contest – for example the eventual runner up, Jessica Verdugo's (Irene Azuela), required speech is a complaint about the bad press her state gets – points to the way the contestants are enlisted as relays of the official truth weapon. In light of Fuentes' above-noted remark that crime has replaced the state, Naranjo takes that reality into the everyday life sphere; he sees his film as a challenge to official attempts to obscure that reality by showing something "unexplored: the secret life of panic, the way that crime invades the everyday and mentally corrodes people who are outside its actions."[60]

Shortly after registering for the contest, Laura is to experience that panic as she learns that the protocols controlling her bodily gestures and speech are minor compared to what she faces when she becomes a pawn of the drug gang. After she and Suzu become qualified contestants, they show up at a nightclub where the gang attacks. That misadventure is what delays Laura's return to the contest headquarters, where she is turned away for missing the appearance time. Although Laura had been allowed to escape after the head of the gang, Lino Valdez (Noe Hernadez) spotted her in the shower; she is later captured by the gang after she begs a transit policeman to help her locate Suzu, who has disappeared after the attack on the club. Instead of helping her, the cop, who turns out to be a collaborator with the gang, delivers her to them. Recognizing her from the club, they hustle her into a van, brutalize and threaten her, and leave her with a hood over her head with Lino, who is to decide her fate.

Throughout that sequence Naranjo's rapidly moving camera gives the viewer a sense of the panic and confusion afflicting Laura as she is swept up in the gang's running battles with authorities. That cinematic style, along with the long takes, show the way she is trapped by creating a sense of her claustrophobia especially when, after she has tried to run away, Lino and his gang occupy her house. Lino, expels her father and brother and forces her to share her bed after having demanded that she get undressed. In the household, Naranjo's visual language articulates the rhythms of light and dark that have altered Laura's domestic sphere, changing it from its day-to-day rhythms of domesticity to the rhythms of dominance and submission. As night turns into day (ambiguously as the play of light versus dark keeps switching), Lino prepares Laura for the delivery of money to the US in order to acquire a new supply of ammunition lost during a police raid on the gang's hideout. Laura's trip to the US side of the border reveals two levels of control and constraint as well as the collection of agencies assembled to make narco-trafficking possible.

The first control is the border policing, a place where typically "danger happens" because ordinarily, as "the boundary between inside and outside [where] the inside is safe, outside is danger."[61] However, in Laura's case, she is leaving one kind of danger behind and facing another, which the viewer sees from Laura's point of view, as on the way north, she passes through the border control in a taxi and responds to a question about the reason for her visit with the remark, "I'm going shopping." The same zoom/framing shot of the border is shown from her point of view on the way back, in heightened danger because she is driving a car full of the ammunition she has purchased on her "shopping trip." The second control is another instance of coercion over Laura's body. The "gringo" who cuts the tape around her waist and takes the money keeps demanding in a surly voice that she keep her hands on the wheel of the car. Although Laura's anxious journey is continuously onscreen, the viewer gets a sense of the network of apparatuses (*dispositifs*) that are the conditions of possibility for the trafficking venture – the money taped to Laura, the taxi driver willing to take the risk, the pilot and plane used to fly her further north, whoever has made the car available for her return trip, and all the persons involved in the US who procure weapons and ammunition to sell to the traffickers: the various officials and agencies that, either through incompetence or corruption, allow the transactions, and the government agencies whose policy priorities direct insufficient attention to the problem.

Back at the beauty contest, we see a Laura who is too traumatized at this point to either smile or make words. When it's her turn to deliver the typical beauty contest platitudes (her opponent, Jessica, who precedes her, says that the beautiful city of Baja deserves respect) she can't make her voice work. She is crowned Miss Baja nevertheless because of the power of the drug gang-policing apparatuses controlling her, and ultimately, as the beauty queen, she is delivered to the military head of the anti-drug initiative, General Duarte, at a hotel gathering, where Lino, who is now collaborating with the army, is pretending to set up an assassination but instead is setting up his own gang (although he too is betrayed and killed before the event is over). For the last time, in the general's room, Laura is told to undress, and when the general begins to caress her, and she whispers that he is about to be murdered, she is told to dress. After the ensuing fire fight in which both gang members and some of the general's guard are killed, Laura becomes the prime sacrifice. The soldiers beat her up, television commentators (including Luisa, the beauty contest coordinator) report her as a disgrace to Mexico as a narco-trafficking collaborator, and she is once again forced into a car and driven away. Bruised and battered, she is let out in a back street warehouse district. As we see her for the last time, it is again from the back. She is the film's primary victim (doubtless representing the Mexican victims of the drug war as a whole). The view from behind her is a visual statement that she has now sunk below the level of recognition. Her moments of special recognition, which had been a contrivance of the main players in the duplicitous war, are over because her body is no longer useful capital for their nefarious projects.

Ultimately, Naranjo's film is a powerful attack on the official discourses of the "war on drugs." *His* weapons are what André Bazin famously calls "image facts"…"fragment(s) of concrete reality," which have the effect of freeing the viewer from the dominant representations of state policy by allowing her/him to connect the fragments of image facts into a narrative coherence that gives the lie to the US–Mexico truth weapons.[62] Although Naranjo's cinematic politics of aesthetics is singular, it has some resonances with Pier Paolo Pasolini's cinematic politics. One way of construing that resonance is to see a Pasolini *interruptus* at work in the way Naranjo's camera moves. While for example, Pasolini explored the dreary life-worlds of the downtrodden classes living on the outskirts of a "Rome, Ringed by its Hell of Suburbs"[63] in his *Mama Rosa* (1962) with a lot of long takes and framing shots of desolate cityscapes and housing projects, Naranjo offers only brief glimpses of the more dreary venues of Baja California. Instead, he creates disrupting blurs of motion, as the actions of the narco-trafficking gang and their policing counterparts (who either oppose or assist their enterprise) disrupt even this mundane and oppressed part of the life-world. We get glimpses of the Pasolini aesthetic, only to have it continually interrupted as Naranjo's camera captures rapidly moving bodies and vehicles. (For example, a fire fight between the gang and the police in which Laura is constantly threatened by the crossfire creates a charged and confusing atmosphere in a grim under-bridge urban scene, which ends when the gang escapes in a huge dump truck).

Having explored cinematic texts that effectively map the extent of the apparatuses involved in the war in drugs, while indicating its the effects on the everyday life-world in Mexico, I want to conclude by raising the question of where justice can be located in a war in which law enforcement is at least as responsible for atrocities as are the drug gangs and in a policy environment in which a new bantustanization is on the agenda.

Justice?

Although it's clear that Laura's experience is traumatic, and her anxiety is palpable, the political force of her experience, as it emerges through her movement trajectory, is better thought if she's rendered as an aesthetic rather than as a psychological subject (a conceptual persona I treat in Chapter 1). By treating Laura as an aesthetic subject, we can look at the way the forces affecting her shape Naranjo's cinematic space, as she is forced to perform within many of the spaces that are the conditions of possibility for narco-trafficking. Laura's movements etch the cartography of the drug trafficking and policing process as they function both as an enterprise and as violent disruptions of much of Mexico's life-world. Although there is a manifest passivity in the way that Laura reacts to her capture within the criminal/policing process, there is nevertheless a "political subjectivization" that she represents as a "subject of rights" (whose rights to free movement) are abridged. She is the kind of political subject who "inscribe(s) the count of the uncounted," where the politics of subjectivity here is about the political qualification of those regarded as unqualified.[64] Thus although Laura herself is passive, Naranjo's film effects a political subjectivization; the force of his cinematic art is what allows Laura to rise above the level of recognition, not only as one who achieves notoriety by winning a beauty contest but also as one who stands for the uncounted within the political discourses of the war on drugs. While generally beauty contests can create instant recognition for those who are largely unnoticed within a system of the social exchange of recognition, in this case the film adds contingency to that kind of recognition event by framing it within a historical moment when extra-state forces are impinging on the society, creating panic, quiescence, and the breakdown and/or corruption of justice implementing agencies whose personnel collaborate with crime organizations.

Thus official proclamations to the contrary, in the "war on drugs" (as the beauty contest coordinator, Luisa says in an earlier quotation), "nothing is fair." The problem to contemplate then is to how to conceive justice, given the facts of complicity between the justice *dispositif*, constituted by the official war on drugs, and the crime *dispositif*, as it unfolds in the process of narco-trafficking. Inasmuch as my focus has been on the diverse apparatuses that are the vehicles of the trafficking and policing, I want to again summon the relevant methodological insight provided by Michel Foucault, (described in Chapter 1) whose remarks on *dispositifs* have established its critical usage, especially in his lectures under the title of *The Birth of Biopolitics*, where, as I noted, Foucault begins with some remarks on his "choice of method," where he remarks, as I noted, "instead of deducing concrete phenomena from universals, or instead of starting with universals as an obligatory grid of intelligibility for certain concrete practices, I would like to start with the concrete practices and, as it were, pass these universals through the grid of these practices."[65]

A focus on the policing practices involved in the war on drugs highlights the injustices. Given the vagaries of policing and the arbitrariness of the way states and their implementing agencies determine licit versus illicit commodities and warrants for their transfers, it turns out that in the war on drugs, "nothing is fair," both in terms of what becomes an object of coercive control and in terms of the extent to which there is protection of the rights of those who live in areas where the drug war is ongoing. Agencies that might otherwise concern themselves with justice-as-fairness, pursue a "justice" that takes the form of violent confrontation.

Are there other options? There is one nation state, Bolivia, which much to the chagrin of US policing agencies, resists the model of justice-as-a-war-on-drugs. In contrast to Mexico's President Felipe Calderon, whose militarization of the policing function had accelerated the death rate in the Mexican drug war, is Bolivian President

Evo Morales' approach. His weapon is "coca licensing" rather than the militarization of the policing function.[66] The context for Morales' approach is the historical subordination of Bolivia's indigenous population whose cultural practices and interests, prior to Morales' presidency, were neglected. Although they had begun to achieve some recognition within a neoliberal development economic paradigm before Morales assumed the presidency, there was no recognition of the moral economy within which many of them worked as coca farmers. Pre Morales governments continued to participate in the global anti-drug initiatives.

After taking office in January of 2006, Morales introduced a different "borderline justice," one based on a different governmentality. In terms of the "borderline," he sharply distinguished coca from its manufactured byproduct, cocaine. And in terms of his altered governmentality, rather than continuing with the prior model in which all citizens were regarded as the same political subjects, he focused on the fault-lines within the Bolivian society that have historically created different interests and alternative moral economies between the Euro-Hispanic and indigenous populations.[67] In effect, Morales turned back the clock to delink coca from contemporary commodity flows and re-enfranchise (pre global capitalist) relationships that had shaped Bolivian society:

> A three-century interregional Spanish colonial coca leaf trail traversed what is now Peru, Bolivia, Chile, and Northern Argentina, largely for mine workers and other hard laborers. It predated the creation of a global taste and market for coca, which only started with the French luxury commodity drink *Vin Maraini* in 1863 and later industrialized during the German medicinal *kocain* boom of 1884–1887.[68]

Intervening on the drug war protection racket, where states have sought to have fiscal control over commodity flows, in 2009, Morales kicked out the agents of the US's

DEA and arrested the former head of the Bolivian anti-narcotics police (on trafficking charges). Those moves were coupled with a strict licensing law applied to coca growing which has led to drop in coca production of 12 to 13 percent along with a drop in the violent crimes that are "the bloody byproduct of American-led measures to control trafficking in Colombia, Mexico and other parts of the region."[69] Although Bolivia under Morales still criminalizes cocaine, it recognizes coca leaf as a traditional medicine/stimulant, chewed by a large percentage of the indigenous population. Registering thousands of growers in the Chapare region, the government limits plantings to make sure of equal access to the product (as well as a fair level of income for growers) while containing its use in trafficking. Without the violence associated with the American paramilitary model, the Morales government has eradicated many acres of coca without anything like the levels of violence that the anti-drug war in Mexico has produced: "A government report said that 60 people were killed and more than 700 wounded in the Chapare from 1998–2002 in violence related to eradication."[70]

"Fair but hard?" Finally, to return to the line from the film narrative in Mann's *T Men*, which implies that the policing apparatus delivers an impartial justice. I want to consider briefly the flaws in the ever-popular rationalistic approach to justice of liberal constitutionalists such as John Rawls and Ronald Dworkin. In his famous (continually adjusting) account of justice as fairness,[71] Rawls privileges a political liberty in which each person would want to be in a society in which she/he has an equal right to a basic liberty that would apply to all and in which social and economic inequalities are in an arrangement that should be to everyone's advantage and are connected to positions and offices that are equally available to all citizens. Also, committed to a Kant-inspired model of public reason, Rawls embraces a democratic imaginary in which equality amounts to an arithmetic sum such that in matters of justice there is an "inexhaustability of representation"

– anyone can be added to the list of those participating in the justice-related deliberation.[72] In effect, Rawls "talks like a state"; in his later writings he argues that justice as fairness is political rather than metaphysical and is evoked in debates about "constitutional matters."[73]

Dworkin perpetuates a similarly liberal model of justice in which equality is the central concept and a political arithmetic is the primary analytic. At the center of his model is an ahistorical "ethical individual," who should be given an equal opportunity. As I have noted,

> Dworkin reduces political equality to the opportunity individuals have to express their political preferences. His failure to recognize the power of discourse is evident in his articulation of the seemingly unproblematic premise that "people have...political preferences"[74] [whereas]...It is more politically perspicuous to say that political preferences have people. By privileging subjective agency as his primary model of political enactment, Dworkin bars access to the entrenched models of political intelligibility [the talk of the state] available to subjects.[75]

With a version of politics that opposes the Rawlsian/Dworkin political imaginary that sustains their liberal model of justice, Jacques Rancière provides a critique of "the typical political arithmetic within which everyone is a subject before the law or has a political preference to be counted along with others. In contrast to 'the arithmetic of shopkeepers and barterers'...Rancière speaks of 'a magnitude that escapes ordinary measurement,' a 'paradoxical magnitude' that escapes a logic that equates the equality of anyone at all with anyone else'."[76] Rancière's version of politics is well suited to the acts of subjectivization inherent in Naranjo's film *Miss Bala* and President Morales' new governmentality. For Rancière, politics is an event in which an action by a part that is uncounted makes an appearance that challenges "the system that creates modes of subjectivization by reordering the significance of the bodies and spaces within which they function.

Naranjo's Laura and Morales' indigenous coca growers are lent justice by being allowed to rise above the threshold of visibility in challenges to the commodity-oriented "racial state" in Morales' case and to the drug control apparatuses of the drug war state in Naranjo's. Morales challenges the law-making violence that divides licit versus illicit drugs. Naranjo challenges the biopolitical/legal order of division of politically qualified versus unqualified bodies. I'll give Jacques Derrida the last words in this chapter: "Justice as law is never exercised without a decision that *cuts*, that divides."[77] However, his words become important again in the last chapter on justice and archives. Derrrida's commitment to an open archive that is always becoming and thus revising the world's will-have-beens inspires much of the way that chapter is shaped.

5
Justice and the Archives

An Archive of Atrocities

Mathias Énard's novel *Zone*, which inspires much of the analysis in Chapter 1, provides an appropriate initiating perspective for the main concern of this chapter as well. To repeat the novel's historical context and drama: The protagonist, Mirković, a reformed Croatian militiaman, narrates the novel in flashbacks while on a train from Milan to Rome to sell an archive (he's carrying in a suitcase) of the atrocities in "the zone" (the Mediterranean area) to the Vatican. As I have put it elsewhere,

> Within the narrative of the train journey, Énard provides an oblique commentary on the politics of the archive. To secure that archive, Mirković handcuffs the suitcase to a bar on his seat. That gesture, along with the convenient symbols supplied by the train's destination, Rome's Termini station, and the suitcase's destination, the Vatican, implies that once they are situated in the archives of political or religious authorities, the records are sealed, locked up, immune from modification...However, as the novel's construction of its plastic aesthetic subject, Mirković...shows, and its testimony to the fragility of historical recollections

and allegiances to which his journey indicates, the archive is never finally secured.[1]

Among the places where a formerly secured archive has been opened to contestation is post apartheid South Africa, where political activists have been militating in behalf of open-access archives. For example, in a commentary on the archive–justice relationship, South African, Verne Harris, urges an opening of archive record-making to the broad participation of a "host of others," [2] especially those who have been traditionally excluded: "The record...is always in the process of being made. And all of us who narrate its meanings and significances, whether we do it in a togetherness of hospitality or in a separateness of insularity, are record makers." He adds that nevertheless, "The harsh reality is that the shape (and the shaping) of record-making is determined by relations of power."[3] Harris' archival ethos and his political observation accord with the well-known archive thinking of Jacques Derrida, who both promotes the opening of archives to an uncertain future and at the same time recognizes the power-related investments that shape them. The archive, Derrida insists, must be oriented by a "spectral messianicity" in its conception,"[4] and while "there is no political power without control of the archive, if not memory, effective democratization can always be measured by this essential criterion: the participation in and access to the archive, its constitution, and its interpretation."[5] Certainly much of the historical trajectory of record-keeping has been done in behalf of structures of power and control, not only over discourses but also over the spaces of their creation and storage. "Archives," as Derrida points out "are only kept and classified under the title of the archive by virtue of a privileged topology. They inhabit this uncommon place, this place of election where law and singularity intersect in privilege."[6] Focusing on the events of discourse involved in the creation of the archive, Foucault also addresses the archive–power relationship: "The archive is first the law of what can be said, the system that governs the appearance of statements as unique events."[7]

The archive–power relationship has both deep historical roots and a sustained trajectory into the present, for example in the archives that have been activated in inquisitions. An "inquisition," which is ordinarily associated with "the term 'Dark Ages,'...is a set of disciplinary procedures targeting specific groups, codified in law, organized systemically, enforced by surveillance, exemplified by severity, sustained over time, backed by institutional power, and justified by a vision of the one true path."[8] Addressing the conditions of possibility for such inquisitions, Cullen Murphy points out that the atrocities associated with inquisitions are sustained practices of persecution that require not only "procedures...for record-keeping, and for retrieving information after records have been compiled and stored [but also]...an ability to send messages across significant distances – and also some capacity to restrict the communications of others." He adds, "there must be a source of power, to ensure enforcement."[9] The "inquisitorial impulse" to which Murphy refers has persisted since the historic religious inquisitions (most famously the Spanish Inquisition). In its current incarnation, an "inquisition" has been elaborated as the post 9/11 "Homeland Security" initiative, which began under President George W. Bush, has been sustained under President Barack Obama, and has resulted in a security *dispositif*, which involves "some 1,271 government organizations and 1,931 private companies...amounting to an 'alternative geography' of America that is [largely] "hidden from view" (according to a Washington Post 2010 report).[10]

Nevertheless, although the surveillance-related archiving associated with the contemporary "Inquisitorial State,"[11] has been secretive and thereby shielded by the government and its security bureaucracy from accountability, in the contemporary condition in which the Internet has democratized commentary on the significance of events in the past, present, and future, the exclusivity of archiving has been dramatically abrogated. The future anteriors – the will-have-beens of state-initiated Draconian security measures – is an ongoing dynamic as they are increasingly open to contestation by would-be (counter) archivists (like the fictional Mirković) as they gain access to data and public media. In the current media technology condition, new state policy-challenging genres of archiving are proliferating, as for example in the case of the WikiLeaks initiative in which a counter archive of records associated with the excesses of the security apparatuses (among which are the details of files on Guantanamo detainees) and in the case of Edward Snowden's leaking of government surveillance practices, both of which have been made public on the Internet.[12] And other counter-official archive productions are increasingly available from diverse artistic genres, for example feature and documentary films and literatures.

In this chapter I heed the condition of the proliferation of alternative archive genres and assess its implications for the relationship between justice and the archives. To create a frame for pursuing those implications, I begin with another fictional archivist, a Kafkaesque, displaced Hungarian, who has strong resonances with Franz Kafka's Sancho Panza. To begin with the novel's patrimony: In a brief parable, "The Truth about Sancho Panza," Kafka offers an ironic twist to Miguel de Cervantes' epic novel, *Don Quixote*:

Without making any boast of it Sancho Panza succeeded in the course of years, by feeding him a great number of romances of chivalry and adventure in the evening and night hours, in so diverting from himself his demon, whom he later called Don Quixote, that this demon thereupon set out, uninhibited, on the maddest exploits, which, however, for the lack of a preordained object, which should have been Sancho Panza himself, harmed nobody. A free man, Sancho Panza philosophically followed Don Quixote on his crusades, perhaps out of a sense of responsibility, and had of them a great and edifying entertainment to the end of his days.[13]

Although the focus of the parable seems to be on Sancho Panza, doubtless what is more important is how the parable thinks about the concept of "truth," which arguably is applied to Sancho Panza's invention to provide a critique of the traditional concept of a timeless truth, i.e., to show that so-called truth is a function of signifying practices, that it's an effect of language. Kafka's parable challenges the usual way of raising truth questions; it suggests that rather than interrogating *what* truth is, the important questions are: whose truth is being dramatized, from what perspective, and to what purpose. It therefore opens the question of the relationship between truth and power (famously associated with the work of Foucault).[14]

Kafka's Sancho Panza is very likely an inspiration for another fictional character, György Korin, the protagonist in László Krasznahorkai's novel *War and War*. Briefly, Korin, a clerk/archivist in an office on the outskirts of Budapest travels to New York with a manuscript of unclear authorship he has "discovered." His stated intention is to interpret and translate it and load it onto the Internet where (he has speculated) it will be part of history's permanent archive. Apart from his geographic migration from Hungary to New York, Korin undergoes symbolic/identity migrations, first from minor archivist working in a records office in what he regards as a peripheral location, to the place he regards as the center of the earth, the contemporary Rome ("why, he asked himself, why spend his time in an archive some two hundred kilometers southwest of Budapest when he could be sitting in the center of the world")[15] and second, migrating from being a marginal, Hungarian to being a New Yorker and at the same time from being a monolingual Hungarian speaker to one using a hybrid language (his Hungarian is increasingly peppered with English words as the narrative progresses). Like Kafka, Krasznahorkai regards intelligibility as an enigma rather than as an unambiguously positive achievement. Every mode of intelligibility operates within a discursive economy. To alight on a meaning is to jump to an arbitrary place that excludes alternatives. Thus as Korin reads and rereads the manuscript (which he seems to be embellishing, but many clues point to the entire narrative as his invention), he finds that there is no clear way to do justice to what it contains. At several points in his rereading, he concedes that he cannot understand the manuscript: for example, "He had read it through countless times...but the manuscript's mystery was by no means diminished..."[16] He nevertheless dedicates himself to "recover the dignity and meaning whose loss he had been mourning," even as he wonders why "it did not respond to the pressure of expectation," was not "a work of literature" (or any familiar genre), and has an ambiguous, "form of address." At a minimum," he surmises, "Its perfectly clear that it was not addressed to anyone in particular."[17] As a result, the novel implies that archiving has no privileged genre and no stable addressee.

Throughout the novel, Krasznahorkai's writing style – long sentences that frequently comprise entire chapters – articulates the manuscript's unusual narrative structure, which follows a journey of four travelers on an Odyssey through both time and space to return home. The journey begins in ancient Minoan Crete, passes through Cologne, Germany in 1812, continues through Venice and then proceeds on to Spain in the fifteenth century. Bracketing for the moment the sentence structure, Korin's rendering of the manuscript constructs it with what M. M. Bakhtin calls "chronotopes" (noted In Chapter 4), which render "the intrinsic connectedness of temporal and spatial relationships that is artistically expressed in literature."[18] In the case of *War and War* the narrative of the manuscript Korin is describing/inventing fits Bakhtin's examples of chronotopes of emergence and encounter. In the former, the "emergence" is dual; it connects the "hero's" individual becoming with a historical becoming, as the person and the world emerge in new forms. With respect to the latter, Bakhtin refers to chronotopes of the road "which is a good place for random encounters...On the road the spatial and temporal series defining human fates and lives combine with one another in distinctive ways, even as they become more complex and more concrete by the collapse of social distances."[19] Thus in addition to destabilizing archives by pluralizing the genres with which they are produced, the novel suggests that the temporality of their production is radically contingent. Louis Althusser's meditation on "the materialism of encounter" captures the contingency of the way Korin accomplishes his archive. Korin's encounter-driven renderings of the manuscript create an archive that involves what Althusser refers to as the alternative creation and displacing of the "accomplished fact": "[Archival] history...is nothing but the permanent revocation of the accomplished fact by an undecipherable fact to be accomplished, without our knowing in advance whether, or when, or how the event that revokes it will come about."[20]

As for the novel's grammatical style, the protagonist helps us appreciate why it has such long sentences. Well into the narrative, Krasznahorkai has Korin speculate on the manuscript's formal structure, which turns out to be homologous with the formal structure of Krasznahorkai's novel as a whole: In Korin's words:

> There is an order in the sentences: words, punctuation, periods, commas all in place...and yet the events that follow in the last chapter may be characterized as a series of collapses...for the sentences have lost their reason, not just growing ever longer and longer but galloping desperately onward in a harum scarum scramble – *crazy rush*...[21]

Krasznahorkai's long sentences gallop along as well; they make the reader present to Korin's musings as Krasznahorkai "draws us toward the consciousness of his archivist character." The vertigo-inducing sentence

structure buttresses Korin's testimony making it evident
that the archivist may well be delusional, while at the same
time demonstrating the vagaries of archival construction
(the ways in which particular forms of memory-as-
invention can constitute what ends up as history). The
novel's grammatical rhythms, delivered in a third personal
narrative, therefore unite the reader with the protagonist,
"offering a stance that is distanced yet remarkably intimate."[22] And crucially, the flow of the sentences, without
interruption, gives the reader an appreciation of all the
aspects of Korin's experience: the ways in which he is
sensing the manuscript, the relevance of how he is dwelling
in the New York life-world (where he is inventing it), and
how his interactions with his interlocutors, a Hungarian
landlord/interpreter and the landlord's abused Puerto
Rican lover/housekeeper, contribute to his interpretations.
The way the novel-as-form develops makes it evident that
rather than *representing* things, the protagonist is *express-
ing* them. As a result, "truth" is not a matter of discovery
but of expression.[23] In what follows, I offer a close reading
of Krasznahorkai's novel in order to derive its implications
for what I am calling the justice of the archives. However
to situate that reading, I turn first to the "method of
dramatization," which shapes my interpretive approach.

The Method of Dramatization

Deleuze's discussion of the method of dramatization is
inaugurated by one of his interlocutors, who identifies
Deleuze's major concern as how to structure the grammar
of questions: "It is not certain that the question *What
is this?* is a good question for discovering the essence or
the Idea."[24] Beginning his response to that provocation,
Deleuze states, "The Idea responds only to the call of
certain questions," and he goes on examine the question-
forms of Platonism: "The question *What is this?* reveals
itself to be confused and doubtful, even in Plato and the

Platonic tradition," Deleuze insists that "The question *What is this?* prematurely judges the Idea as simplicity of the essence..."[25] Resisting such a representational mode of questioning, Deleuze seeks to recover what he calls the dynamisms at work in concepts such as truth and justice. He evokes "a strange theater" in which "a drama...corresponds to this or that concept,"[26] and adds that "pure spatio-temporal dynamisms have the power to dramatize *concepts*, because in the first place they actualize or incarnate *Ideas*."[27] What then is the appropriate grammar for such dramatization? Inspired by Nietzsche's suggestion that rather than asking what something is, we should ask who is interpreting it and from what perspective, Deleuze puts it this way:

> ...when Nietzsche asks *who*, or *from what perspective*, instead of *what*, he is not trying to complete the question *what is this?*, he is criticizing the form of this question and all its possible responses. When I ask *what is this?*, I assume there is an essence behind appearances, or at least something ultimate behind the masks. The other kind of question, however, always discovers other masks behind the mask, displacements behind every place, other 'cases' stacked up in a case.[28]

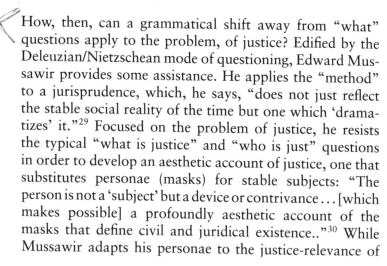

How, then, can a grammatical shift away from "what" questions apply to the problem, of justice? Edified by the Deleuzian/Nietzschean mode of questioning, Edward Mussawir provides some assistance. He applies the "method" to a jurisprudence, which, he says, "does not just reflect the stable social reality of the time but one which 'dramatizes' it."[29] Focused on the problem of justice, he resists the typical "what is justice" and "who is just" questions in order to develop an aesthetic account of justice, one that substitutes personae (masks) for stable subjects: "The person is not a 'subject' but a device or contrivance... [which makes possible] a profoundly aesthetic account of the masks that define civil and juridical existence.."[30] While Mussawir adapts his personae to the justice-relevance of what he regards a practical, personal jurisprudence, I turn to Krasznahorkai's conceptual persona, Korin, to develop politics of archival justice.

Korin

Krasznahorkai's Korin is by his own admission losing his identity coherence as his work on the manuscript proceeds; he's a disintegrating persona: "something in me is breaking up and I'm getting tired."[31] Rather than turning inward, he aggressively externalizes his fractured self. In Jacques Lacan's words, he "throw[s] back on the world the disorder of which his being is composed."[32] Nevertheless, Korin is not a static self. Early in the novel, after he gets to New York, he refers to himself as a "head-archivist-in-waiting"[33] with a lot to do to prepare himself for the task, not the least of which is acquiring and becoming competent with a computer. Lacking facility in English, Korin has his Hungarian landlord/interpreter, Mr Sarvary, accompany him to one of New York's most venerable (if not immortal) institutions, 47th Street Photo, to buy a computer because he has concluded that the internet is the best place to enter a text that you want archived permanently: "For the first time in history," Korin thinks, "the so-called Internet offered a practical possibility of immortality, for there were so many computers in the world by then that computers were for all practical purposes indestructible [and]...that which is indestructible must perforce be immortal."[34]

Korin's musings on the Internet resonate with his perspective on New York as the new Rome, the implication being that the Internet is a better place than the Vatican archive to secure the immortality of the text. Doubtless that is the case in part because the open access of the Internet implicates countless witnesses to the documents, whereas the Vatican archive has opened itself very slowly and with various hindrances to access. After Pope Leo XIII opened the archives for scholars in 1881, a time in which the "opening was intertwined with Italian politics," access was afflicted thereafter by ecclesiastical conflicts associated with the papacy. The apparatuses of archival management hindered access then and has frequently done so since; for example there has been a reluctance of Vatican archive managers (the *archons*) to grant access to researchers who have wanted to investigate Pope Pius XII's attitude toward and behavior during the Holocaust,[35] and they have been reluctant to open the archives on inquisitions (finally doing so in 1998 during the Papacy of John Paul II).[36]

While the Internet, the ultimate venue for Korin's discovered/invented manuscript, has implications for a discernment the politics of archiving, the venues of its preparation are arguably even more telling with respect to the contingencies of archiving. The relevance of the spatial Odysseys of an archivist becomes evident as the novel progresses. While working on the manuscript, Korin is also in the process of inventing himself as an American and as a New Yorker. He is a becoming subject, one who is "axiologically yet-to-be."[37] To do justice to the manuscript and its archiving, he has to invent a just self as well. With respect to his America location, the novel describes it succinctly: "He had become quite a different person in America."[38]

That difference is largely a function of Korin's self-fashioning/self-destruction (a being-toward-death) that he has decided to embrace. At one point he enquires as to whether "the entire notion of America had ultimately come about as a result of his decision to put an end to his life" (once the archiving is competed).[39] With respect to his more specific location, his first New York experiences make him delirious: "The traffic made him dizzy...he was in constant fear of assault at every road and traffic sign."[40] At this stage, Korin is prey to the dizzying effect that Georg Simmel famously describes in his analysis of the way the "metropolis" affects "mental life." It induces a vertigo resulting from "The rapid crowding of changing images, the sharp discontinuity in the grasp of a single glance, and the unexpectedness of onrushing impression. These are the psychological conditions which the metropolis creates. With each crossing of the street, with the tempo and multiplicity of economic, occupational and social life, the city sets up a deep contrast to small town and rural life with reference to the sensory foundations of modern life."[41]

However, as Korin continues exploring the city on foot, urban impressions become increasingly a stimulus to critical reflection rather than a cause of vertigo, as for example at one point when he "journeyed further and further into the heart of town...[and] odd small details, the apparently insignificant parts of the whole...struck him...he felt most intensely that he should be seeing something that he wasn't seeing, that he should be comprehending something he was not comprehending..."[42] He thus increasingly becomes the urban persona that Walter Benjamin famously describes, a "*flaneur*" who is busy "botanizing on the asphalt" rather than the delirious one suggested by Simmel. As Korin continues to read the city, it inflects the way he reads the manuscript; the city turns him into a lexical *flaneur*.[43] Rather than a disruption to mental life, the city, "as a kind of force field of passions that associate and pulse bodies in particular ways,"[44] helps to create the conditions of possibility for a critical mental life. It stimulates Korin's interpretive work as he reads and rereads (or likely invents) the manuscript he has decided to submit to the permanent archive of the Internet.

The novel implicates yet another spatial determinant of Korin's creativity. The architecture of the apartment in which he dwells affects his reading/inventing process. On the one hand there is the privacy of his room where Korin enters the manuscript into his computer file; on the other there is the apartment's kitchen – effectively the apartment's public sphere – where he attempts to communicate his insights about the manuscript to "the woman," the lover/housekeeper of the "interpreter"/landlord (or perhaps better, house lord). Moreover, the various doors and walls

aid his work process; they allow him to avoid the censori-
ous presence of the interpreter, who inhibits his attempt at
"publicity," occasionally attempting to bar his access to
the woman/interlocutor with whom Korin needs to communicate what he is thinking in order to validate his
reading/interpretation of the manuscript. For example:

> He had read it through countless times, thought Korin as
> he sat in the kitchen next day – when, after a long period
> of silence behind the door, he judged that the interpreter
> must be out of the way – for really, he had been through
> it at least five, maybe as much as ten times, but the manu-
> script's mystery was by no means diminished...even as he
> continued devouring the pages...the mystery obscured by
> the unknowable and inexplicable was more important than
> anything else...by now impossible to shake he felt no great
> need to try to explain his own actions to himself, to ask
> why he should have dedicated the last few weeks of his life
> to this extraordinary labor, since what after all did it
> consist of he asked the woman rhetorically...[45]

In effect, the apartment where Korin dwells is one of the
novel's protagonists. More than merely an inert physical
structure, it shapes the way Korin creates the manuscript
as the novel has him in a spatial Odyssey from room to
room. It becomes evident that his becoming as an archivist
is a drama that is dynamically shaped within the apartment as well as in the city. Thus the spatial framing of
Korin's archiving helps to specify what Deleuzian method
identifies as the drama in the concept of archives that the
novel develops. First, there is the protagonist, Korin, whose
antics elaborate the "who" of the archive creation (where
who is interpreting must trump the "what" of the archiving). Then, there is the theater, the spaces involved in the
staging of the interpretation. Although Korin is arguably
crazy, he is best construed not as a "psychological subject"
but as an "aesthetic subject", whose spatial Odyssey is
more important than his state of mind (a conceptual orientation I derive from Leo Bersani and Ulysses Dutoit's

analysis of the characters in Jean Luc Godard's film *Contempt* (1963), as I note in previous chapters).

Although Korin's mental condition is monitored throughout the novel (among other things his plan to end his life once his task is completed), the narrative is intensely involved in both the spaces of Korin's manuscript interpretation (where he *is* from moment to moment as he works on it) and the spatial Odyssey of the manuscript's characters. The novel turns the world into an interpretation-inspiring stage, which shapes the way the archiving drama unfolds as a work of the venue-inspired "creative imagination" of Korin.[46] Certainly the political subjectivity that Korin is acquiring throughout the novel is as much a part of his performance as is the manuscript he is creating to submit to the archive.

However, two aspects of the novel's voice must be appreciated to heed the archive drama unfolding. First, in addition to apprehending Korin as a lexical *flaneur*, we must recognize his "audiography," a concept that emerges in a tracing of the spaces in which Michel Foucault responded orally to queries about his historico-philosophical works. The "audiography is...associated with a number of physical locations. Some are institutional and expected – the university auditorium or radio studio – others are more incongruous" – for example the exchange on intellectuals and power which took place in a conversation with Gilles Deleuze and others in the kitchen of Gilles and Fanny Deleuze in Paris..." As the summary of the tracing puts it, "This geography has left its imprint in the archives."[47] As is the case with discerning the significance of Foucault's remarks in various interviews and recorded conversations, to grasp the significance of the *where* of the way Korin adds an entry to the archive, we need to heed the geography of the language events that add up to its content – Korin in the kitchen of New York apartment, verbalizing to a non-comprehending interlocutor, what he understands (or fails to understand) about the manuscript.

Second, the rhythms of Krasznahorkai's novel articulate a phenomenology of perception – for example in this passage on the beauty of a flight attendant who helps Korin get his visa papers so he can board his plane to New York. Although the passage may seem to be an irrelevant aside, it is exemplary:

> The nipples delicately pressed through the warm texture of the snow-white starched blouse while deep *decollage* boldly accentuated the graceful curvature and fragility of the neck, the gentle valleys of the shoulders and the light swaying to and fro of the sweetly compact masses of her breasts, although it was hard to tell whether it was these that drew the eyes inexorably to her, that refused to let the eyes escape, or it was the short dark-blue skirt that clung to her hips...that arrested them; in other words men and women caught in the moment... – they stared quite openly, the men with crude, long-suppressed hunger and naked desire, the women with a fine attention to the accumulation of detail...dizzy with sensation but, driven by a malignant jealousy at the heart of their fierce inspection...[48]

This seeming aside on how beauty achieves its effects – beauty as a drama of encounter – is illustrative. It serves as a preview of the phenomenological density of the parallel simultaneous texts – Krasznahorkai's and Korin's – which treat the ways in which the creation of the history of war archives is a function of events of encounter, the interactive dramas through which the archives have been assembled as archiving subjects to confront Others whose presence disrupts the tendency toward a proprioceptive (non-reciprocal) relationship to the world. Thus in *War and War* there is a dual dramatic narrative, one involving the encounters that shape the archivist's (Korin's) work of reading and inscription and the other, the contrived encounters of the characters in the manuscript, which shape their tale as they serve as aesthetic subjects in a chronotope of historical encounter. In that narrative, the protagonists report on the history of war's atrocities. They come to recognize (as a result of an encounter with an interlocutor Masterman) that "the spirit of humanity is the spirit of war," for example "the triumph of Koniggratz, or rather the hell of Koniggratz as anyone would say had they witnessed the Prussian victory on that notorious July 3 three years ago, a victory bought at the price of forty-three thousand dead, and that was just the Austrian casualties..."[49] And they ponder (through Korin's interpretation) the means of security or defense in the vast scheme of life's desires and motives:

> ... *the primary level of human*, said Korin – lay in the longing for security, an unquenchable thirst for pleasure, a crying need for property and power and the desire to establish freedoms beyond nature [and]...to offer security in the face of defenselessness, to provide shelter against aggression...the creation of peace instead of war...[50]

What Krasznahorkai's novel, with its non-linear historical dynamic, instructs about the temporal-sensitivity of the genres of archiving warrants pursuing.

The Genres and Temporality of the Archives

In his analysis of Bergsonism, Gilles Deleuze writes, "[O]f the present we must say at every instant that it 'was,' and of the past, that it 'is'."[51] The manuscript that Korin is submitting to the Internet archive is a patchwork of historical shards. Instead of a linear history of the events of war and postwar experiences, the protagonists bring the past into evolving presents, a "Bergsonism" that encourages reflection on the implications of reliving the past in light of subsequent events. Another way of conceiving the approach to war that the novel's temporal tropes express is afforded by Walter Benjamin's notion of "temporal plasticity." Reflecting on the poetry of Friedrich Hølderlin, Benjamin refers to what he calls a "plastic structure of thought, "[52] It is a "temporal plasticity,"[53] a time "wholly without direction. "[54] Benjamin's notion of temporal plasticity articulates with the ethos of historical sensibility that he promotes, a history that permits new beginnings instead of being seen as "a sequence of events like the beads of a rosary."[55]

What kind of new beginning can emerge from the way the novel *War and War* treats history and archiving? In the process of doing justice to the manuscript he has discovered/invented, Korin is in effect seeking an archival justice. Inasmuch as the drama of Korin's work is literary rather than juridical, we should address the contrast for which Shoshana Felman (cited in earlier parts of this book) provides the relevant gloss. To repeat it: After posing the question, "What indeed is literary justice, as opposed to legal justice?" she answers, "Literature is a dimension of concrete embodiment and a language of infinitude that in contrast to the language of the law, encapsulates not closure but precisely what in a given legal case refuses to be closed and cannot be closed. It is to this refusal of the trauma to be closed that literature does justice."[56] Indicating the ways in which justice responds to the theatricality of the trial, she adds, "...the body of the witness is the ultimate site of memory of individual and collective trauma [as a result]...trials have become not only memorable discursive scenes, but dramatically physical theaters of justice."[57]

We are thus positioned to recall Deleuze's methodological injunction, "Given any concept, we can always discover its drama,"[58] and are encouraged, more specifically to reflect on the drama of the archives. While the courtroom constitutes a drama that is ultimately closural, literature, as Felman insists, resists closure. Felman's position is very well illustrated in the case of South Africa, which has produced, on the one hand a truth and reconciliation commission, and on the other a rich literature that reflects on the identities of persecutors and victims. For example, Gillian Slovo's post-apartheid South African novel *Red Dust*, focused mainly on an encounter between a former torturer/interrogator Dirk Hendricks and his victim Alex Mpondo, offers a more complex reading of the persons involved in committing atrocities than tends to emerge in trial transcripts. Hendricks has applied for an amnesty to the Truth and Reconciliation Commission and must manage a particular identity/impression to achieve credibility (he has to appear contrite and as one who, as a torturer, was merely professional rather than sadistic). While at such trials, the task of the court is to decide which he is, a literary approach is open to the ambiguity and dividedness of identities. The novel provides a variety of Hendricks, e.g., this one seen from Alex Mpondo's (one of his victims) point of view as he interrogates him: "Looking across the space that separated them, Alex found himself looking at a stranger. The man who sat opposite him was not the torturer who had haunted his life: he was just an ordinary man brought down by history and by the compulsion to grab history's second chance and cross the line from instigator to applicant, from perpetrator to reconciled...the man whom Alex had known...seem to have vanished. Dirk Hendrick's grey eyes...surely weren't grey like that before..."[59]

As the interrogation proceeds, "the new Dirk Henricks was still too firmly ensconced to let loose the other" until Mpondo mentions Hendrick's estranged wife: "the mention of the wife: in the flashing of the stranger's eyes was a glimmer of the other."[60] The novel does not help the reader decide if Hendricks is a liar, a problem that the tribunal would have to solve. Rather it leaves open the issue in order to render identities and relationships ambiguous and to treat the issue of the atrocities by the white apartheid regime's functionaries experientially by pondering the emotional damage to both perpetrators and victims. And yet another perpetrator, Pieter Muller, is described as a split person by his wife, Marie, who to her own financial disadvantage testifies that his death was a suicide, not to save his black antagonist who has been cajoled by Muller into shooting him, but to save a version of Pieter. She says, "what I did I did for him... for Pieter. For his memory... I couldn't let that Pieter [the crafty violent version] win... the lie I told was in memory of that good man... the man Pieter had been. The man he might have been."[61] As the narrative proceeds, another main protagonist, Sarah Barcant, a lawyer who had left South Africa for New York before returning to help with the amnesty cases, learns that both justice and truth are too complex to be settled by a tribunal. She says, "If the new rulers of South Africa think justice is complicated, well, they should know that the truth is even more elusive."[62] In effect, the literary archive, of which Slovo's novel is a part, is establishing an alternative to legal justice, an archive of continuous reflection rather than one of definitive judgment. That archive contrasts with the presumption of those who, focusing on legal discourse, analyze tribunals in search of definitive judgments about truth and justice. Slovo's novel points to interpretive ambiguities and thus to contestability of those concepts.

We can turn again to Énard's novel *Zone* where that same contrast is enacted. In a playful passage (cited in Chapter 1), describing the war crimes trial, Énard writes:

> ... in the Great Trial organized by the international lawyers immersed in precedents and the jurisprudence of horror, charged with putting some order into the law of murder, with knowing at one instant a bullet in the head was a legitimate *de jure* and at what instant it constituted a grave breach of the law and customs of war... peppering their verdicts with flowery Latin expressions, devoted, yes, all these people to distinguishing the different modes of crimes against humanity before saying gentlemen I think we'll all adjourn for lunch... the Chamber requests the parties to postpone the hearings planned for this afternoon until a later date, let's say in two months, the time of the law is like that of the church, you work for eternity...[63]

However, Énard himself is not, like the lawyers, "immersed in precedents and the jurisprudence of horror." Like Krasznahorkai, he creates the drama of a becoming archivist in order to create a counter effectuation of the official archives of atrocity. His novel thus encourages a more open archive. At the same time that his protagonist is becoming an archivist, as he heads toward Rome to deliver the catalogue of atrocities in his briefcase, the novel offers a series of glosses on the role of writers who evince a "literary justice" bringing the past into various presents. In the process of exploring the history of atrocity in the "zone," Énard creates a literary archive that contains the fiction writers whose texts explore issues of atrocity and justice: Apollinaire, Butor, Homer, Joyce, and Pynchon, and the canonical fictional responses to war and atrocities by Joseph Conrad, Ernest Hemingway, and Ezra Pound, among others. Many of these latter writers were personally affected by a history of violence in the "zone."

I want to call particular attention to Conrad because the route he took, which inspired his anti-colonialism, has influenced a powerful recovery of the injustices visited on Africa by colonial powers. Conrad's route was retraced by the Swedish writer/activist Sven Lindqvist, in order to tell the story of the extermination of much of Africa's native population by Europeans in the nineteenth century. Fashioning himself as an aesthetic subject, Lindqvist articulates a literary justice as he visits the extermination sites to reflect on the violent nineteenth century European-African encounters, while at the same time including the archival testimony that rehearses the rationales used to justify the slaughters.[64] Lindqvist's work is one genre among many within which the past has been drawn into the present in order to seek justice for victims whose experiences have not had extensive coverage in official archives and/or in juridical venues.

In effect, Lindqvist fashions himself as one of justice's conceptual personae. He enters the historical drama by reliving an era of atrocity and blending his own creative imagination with shards from the historical record. He fashions his journey as a narrative of a man [Lindqvist] traveling by bus through the Sahara Desert while simultaneously traveling by computer through the history of the concept of extermination. Krasznahorkai's Korin – simultaneously doing justice to the manuscript he is entering into the Internet and to moments in the history of war through his four personae who see "only war and war everywhere"[65] – also exercises a creative imagination which he commits to his computer: "...the manuscript that preoccupied him was a work of art of the highest caliber, so he was very much in a position to understand the problems of the creative imagination..."[66]

What would a just archive be with respect to histories of atrocity, and what aspects expressed in what genres can recover the dramas that open the archives of justice that official institutions have tended to fetishize (where a fetishized archive is one that is inanimate rather than historically mobile)? Part of the issue is addressed in Adam Gopnik's reflections on academic responsibility. Referring to what "we" as academics owe to such histories in response to suggestions that the histories contain "a sense of proportion," he writes:

> Whatever academic scholarship may insist, surely a sense of proportion is the last thing we want from history – perspective certainly, not proportion. Anything, after all, can be seen in proportion, shown to be no worse a crime than some other thing. Time and distance can't help but give us a sense of proportion: it was long ago and far away and so what? What great historians give us instead, is a renewed sense of sorrow and anger and pity for history's victims.[67]

While I endorse Gopnik's suggestion (although I am more partial to the contributions of artists and writers than to "great historians"), I want to emphasize two significant aspects of Krasznahorkai's *War and War*: its turn to the Internet as the space of archives and its spatio-temporality. With respect to the former, of late reality is imitating

Krasznahorkai's fiction. On March 8th, 2013, *The Jerusalem Post* reported that France had released and placed on the Internet the documents from one of history's most dramatic trials, the trial of Alfred Dreyfus, the French Jewish artillery officer wrongfully accused of spying for Germany in 1894.[68] Without going into the sordid details of the case (after years in prison, Dreyfus was exonerated and reinstated in the army as a Lieutenant-Colonel in 1906), I want to again evoke the difference between legal and literary justice. Whereas the French courtroom had closed the Dreyfus case with a verdict, French writers had kept the case open. In addition to Emile Zola's well-known *J'accuse*, an open letter in 1898 in a French newspaper, accusing the government of anti-Semitism while pointing to flaws in the court's procedures and evidence collection (ultimately forcing the writer into temporary exile), I want to call attention to Anatole France's satiric novel *Penguin Island* (1908), which ridicules the evidentiary process used by the military against Dreyfus. Using a pseudonym for Dreyfus and the accusing army officers, France has a "General Panther," state "with patriotic satisfaction...proofs against Pyrot [Dreyfus]?...We had not got them when we convicted him, but we have plenty of them now."[69] And "Six months later the proofs against Pyrot filled two storeys of the Ministry of War [and were so heavy that] the ceiling fell in beneath of weight of the bundles, and the avalanche of falling documents crushed two head clerks..."[70]

What Anatole France achieves with satiric irony is expressed by Achille Mbembe analytically in a meditation on the spatio-temporality of archives. Noting that "the term archives refers to a building, a symbol of a public institution," and to "a collection of documents – normally written documents – kept in this building," Mbembe surmises that, "the status and power of the archive derive from this entanglement of building and documents."[71] It is the material presence of archive buildings that effects the power-invested, identification and consolidation of the diverse documents constituting the archive (what Derrida refers to as its "consignation)"[72]

Turning to the second aspect of *War and War*, its "plastic temporality," I want to call attention to the way treatments of ongoing war atrocities in artistic texts have the effect of rethinking those in the past. For example in her *Hiroshima after Iraq*, Rosalyn Deutsche provides specific cases that speak to the implications of Benjamin's concept of plastic temporality. She analyzes how to rethink the bombing of Hiroshima now that the US's Iraq invasions are part of the historical archive of war. Highlighting the critical temporality that derives from the grammatical tense that locates the past in the future – the future anterior (the will-have-been) – she dwells on the significance of several returns to Hiroshima. In one example, she analyzes Silvia Kolbowski's video *After Hiroshima Mon Amour*, which "returns to Hiroshima to confront the legacy of the atomic bombing, linking it to the present invasion and occupation of Iraq."[73] Recasting the Duras/Resnais film, *Hiroshima Mon Amour* (1959) by using a different temporal pacing and different mode of oral address, while including images from Iraq, Kolbowski's heterogeneous temporal association of the two wars gives both the past and the present different interpretive significance. It is one artistic event among many in which the arts participate in challenging the official archive of war. Summing up the significance of Kolbowski's temporal inter-articulation of the Hiroshima bombing and the Iraq invasion and occupation, Deutsche writes, "The word *after* in Kolbowski's title raises the question of time and therefore of history, which is to say of the meaning of past events."[74]

Doubtless the drama of the archives of war that Deutsche rehearses in her survey of the arts is what is accomplished in Krasznahorkai's *War and War*. The novel is a critical response to the temporally oriented questions and suggestions about archives that Derrida has explored. After focusing on the "when" rather than the "what" of archives, Derrida states, "I asked myself what is the moment *proper* to the archive."[75] Like Deutsche, Derrida evokes the future anterior: "The archive: if we want to know what that will have meant, we will only know in times to come."[76] And like Krasznahorkai's Korin, Derrida heeds the new technologies that give the archive its current "moment" as well as its *where*: "The technical structure of the *archiving* archive determines the structure of the *archivable* content...email is privileged...because electronic mail today, even more than fax, is on the way to transforming the entire public and private space of humanity" (i.e. the theater of the archiving drama is increasingly the Internet).[77] Also like Korin, Derrida's evocation of the Internet responds to the question about doing justice to the archives. As he puts it, the archive must partake of "a responsibility for tomorrow."[78] It is in this sense that he, like Krasznahorkai, renders the justice of the archive as a historical drama.

Yet Another Archive Drama

Hidden archives often make their presence known through encounters. In this section I want to analyze the accidental discovery of another archive drama, one that articulates the kind of counter-temporality to which Rosalyn Deutsche gestures in her thinking about historical status of the Hiroshima bombing after the Iraq War. Because of the space of its creation, it challenges the familiar ensemble of building and document collection model of official archives that Mbembe has noted. As is well known, the Enola Gay, the plane that dropped the Atom Bomb on Hiroshima, is part of the US national archive. It is located in the Aeronautical and Space Museum, which is part of the Smithsonian Institute complex. In 1994 as the museum prepared to exhibit the B-29 aircraft and include alternative narratives of the consequences of the bombing, an article in the April 1994 issue of *Air Force Magazine* attacked the plan for being "political" rather than merely "aeronautical."

Stirred to action by the article, members of Congress became self-appointed *archons* of the archive and blocked the inclusion of the narratives.

But there are other archival venues that offer political challenges to the building/document complex that would fetishize the Hiroshima bombing as merely part of an effective military strategy (to be interpreted merely in connection with the history of flight). To identify another archival genre that treats the Hiroshima bombing while at the same time recalling the analytic I am applying to the politics of archival dramas, – where the focus is not on *what* but rather *where* and from *whose perspective* the archive is constituted – I introduce an alternative to the museum as an archival venue and an unofficial archivist, a homeless artist, who was discovered living on a street (6th Avenue) in Lower Manhattan, Jimmy Mirikitani, the protagonist of the documentary film, *The Cats of Mirikitani*.[79] The director/documentary maker of the film, Linda Hattendorf, lived very near the place where Jimmy created and occasionally sold his drawings. Passing him frequently and fascinating by his drawings of cats, she decided to do a short film interview with him.

> It was January 2001, and bitterly cold. He was wrapped in so many hats, coats, and blankets that I could barely see his face. Despite the cold, he was proudly exhibiting his artwork under the shelter of a Korean deli. A picture of a cat caught my eye and we struck up a conversation. It was soon apparent that he was not just selling his artwork, but homeless and living on the street. He seemed so old and frail, and yet full of spirit and life. I was curious and concerned – and I like cats. He gave me the drawing, but asked me to take a picture of it for him. I came back the next day with a small video camera. I asked if he could tell me the stories in some of his pictures. And he had many stories to tell! That's how it began.[80]

The "stories to tell" turned out to powerfully inflect an event that took place during Hattendorf's documentary.

Born in Sacramento, California and raised in Hiroshima, Jimmy and his family experienced two kinds of war atrocity. First, despite being an American citizen, born in Sacramento, he like many Americans of Japanese ancestry was sent to an internment camp. Held there for nearly four years, he was forced to sign a document renouncing his citizenship and was then held for brief periods in two other places – effectively forced labor camps – before he ended up in New York and in the street, after the man for whom he worked as a domestic servant died. Added to his being victimized with his illegal incarceration, the Hiroshima bombing wiped out much of his family in Japan.

Recording in his drawings the atrocities visited on him and his family, Jimmy was a practicing archivist. Depicted in some of his drawings are the Tule Lake, California detention site (for example this one in Image 27) and the Hiroshima bombing (Image 28). Among the various implications of the Jimmy Mirikitani archive, is where it existed – in the street – before Hattendorf's film expanded its publicity, bringing it to cinema screens. Thus, while the Enola Gay exhibition has been in a building (part of what Derrida in an above citation referred to as a "privileged topology") that has protected its bombing mission from challenge and interpretive renegotiation, Jimmy's has been in the street, a place that has often provided spaces of contestation and renegotiation of the meanings of events. His life and work constitute a challenge to the entrenched, allegiance-affirming, archived versions of US policy toward the domestic and foreign Japanese during the Second World War.

The street is often an archival space for contestation over historical memory. For example, in Prague, in the Czech Republic, the archive of the Russian military missions to suppress Czech independence movements (one successful and one not) exists on the city's main thoroughfare, *Vaclavske nam*. When Soviet tanks invaded on August 21, 1968, the bullets fired from the tanks left pockmarks in the national museum just above the main icon on the

Images 27 and 28: Tule Lake and the Hiroshima bombing

street, a statue of King Wenceslas. The archive of the attack is not *in* a building; it is *on* one and is thus visible from the street. The Czechs preserve the memory of the attack by leaving those pockmarks on the building. Subsequently, that same street became another kind of archival space. On November 17, 1989 *Vaclavske nam* was the main site of protest (as part of what came to be known as the "Velvet Revolution" that freed Czechoslovakia from Soviet domination). That event is continually marked by flowers, which are laid at the foot of the Wenceslas statue.[81]

As significant as where Jimmy's archives have been located is the historical moment of their discovery. While the documentary was underway, a momentous event intervened, the 9/11 destruction of the World Trade Center buildings. As Hattendorf testifies:

> Jimmy had lost homes in such a profound way in the past, through war and discrimination; I wanted to explore how this may have contributed to him winding up homeless on the streets 60 years later...Then in September, the attack on the World Trade Center changed life as we knew it in lower Manhattan. I found I couldn't just stand there watching dispassionately through the lens of the camera as Jimmy coughed in the smoke. I brought my subject home – breaking all kinds of rules about objectivity in filmmaking![82]

Incorporating the event into the making of the documentary, Hattendorf gave the *when* of Jimmy's archive special significance. As her filming proceeded, after taking Jimmy into her home, the documentary inter-articulates the atrocities experienced by Jimmy and his family with the post 9/11 securitization and the demonization of Arab Americans. Making use of the advantages of the cinema genre, which can actualize a contingent mode of time through its "yoking together of noncontiguous spaces with parallel editing" to effect a "disfiguration of continuous time,"[83] the documentary effects a temporal montage, showing shots of the towers still standing, of the towers burning, of Jimmy's drawings, of the television news reporting episodes of suspicion about the loyalty of Arab Americans, of aspects of President Bush's war on terror initiatives, and of a newspaper headline, "Past Recalled for Japanese Americans," all of that interspersed with Jimmy's comments: "take house, everything – God damn, born Sacramento, California...This is history you know...120,000 of us out here illegally," "same old story," (at a moment when the camera zooms in on Jimmy's Hiroshima bombing drawing) "can't make war – ashes, everything ashes." And at one point, Hattendorf edits in a television voice saying, "History tells us we have often reacted in time of fear by overreacting."

Ultimately however, although the documentary dwells on the securitization *dispositif* (the apparatuses and discourses of security), Hattendorf's initiatives, once she enters the documentary to take care of Jimmy – getting in touch with a variety of persons and agencies that restore his citizenship papers, reuniting him with the sister he had lost track of for 60 years, getting him an apartment and a pension, and bringing him on a tour back to the Tule Lake detention center to connect with other victims – her efforts result in the formation of a temporary justice *dispositif*, which includes not only the documentary but also the apparatuses mobilized to restore much of what Jimmy had lost. That *dispositif* consists of the entire cinema organization, and the welfare agencies, the media used to track lost and/or distant relatives, the Social Security Administration, and all the other agencies that Linda recruited to change Jimmy's status.

Where in this tale is justice? It's in the film genre and in the *dispositif* that the filmmaking created – the various persons and agencies that involved themselves in both revealing Jimmy Mirikitani's archive and honoring and redeeming him as an artist/archivist. Ultimately, the documentary lends justice a "symphonic temporality;" it allows a past to be "imaginatively reclaimed" in the context of a way of thinking about the present.[84]

Migrant Archives

Clearly the dominant story of official archives is a nation-state story. As Rodrigo Lazo puts it, "The history of the modern archive is inextricable from the establishment of nation-states…Archive and nation came together to grant each other authority and credibility."[85] However, as he adds, "A personal archive has the potential to challenge the authority of the national building."[86] Such a personal archive has been created by migrant Cambodian American culture producers who "reimagine *alternative* nonhegemonic sites for justice [in a variety of genres]...film, literature, hip-hop, and visual culture."[87] Among those culture producers are two young Cambodian American women, Loung Ung and Chanrithy Him, whose retellings of "contrapuntal childhood moments" during the Cambodia genocide offer alternative "cartographies [of] culpability."[88] In contrast to the macropolitical archival sites through which official memories are enacted and fixed as displays within buildings – for example the former high school-turned-security-prison (Tuol Sleng), which has been turned yet again into a museum destination for "dark tourism" – are their micropolitical memories of specific sites where they witnessed atrocities, now recorded in their writing. For example Ung writes, "While children elsewhere in the world watched TV, I watched public executions. While they played hide-and-seek with their friends, I hid in bomb shelters with mine. When a bomb hit and killed my friend Pithy, I brushed her brains off my sleeve."[89] Such nomadic loci of enunciation constitute a perspectival challenge to statist reconciliation discourses and institutionalized sites of memory, designed to reestablish the authority of governance. In contrast, the experiential writing of Ung and Him are discourses and sites designed to seek justice. And Patricia Schlund-Vials' book, which reports the justice-relevant writings of Ung and Him, while reviewing diverse culture productions, effectively stages an encounter between two post-genocide productions, the official/institutional and the affective/experiential. It reopens what official institutional practices attempt to close, summoning our attention to war crimes, atrocities and the issue of justice in the face of institutionalized and individual/phenomenological modes of distraction.

By way of conclusion – for this chapter and my investigation as a whole – I want to emphasize what has been involved as I have invited literary productions and testimonies into the historical archive that bears on the politics of justice. Jacques Rancière raises a relevant question and suggests an answer:

> A well-known Aristotelian sentence says that human beings are political because they own the power of speech that puts into common the issues of justice and injustice while animals only have voice to express pleasure or pain. It could seem to follow from this that politics is the public discussion on matters of justice among speaking people who are all able to do it. But there is a preliminary matter of justice: How do you recognize that the person who is mouthing a voice in front of you is discussing matters of justice rather than expressing his or her private pain?[90]

The "preliminary" question to which Rancière refers opens the question of a politics of recognition. While the proceedings of tribunals must be involved with selecting specific, indictable perpetrators and specific evidence-worthy testimony, the literary archive that has occupied my attention opens the problem of justice to an ethico-political negotiation in which the list of potentially qualified participants cannot be closed. The additional question I want to emphasize has to do with our responsibility to those who have yet to be heard. The narrator of Zadie Smith's story, which I cite in the Introduction, evokes the relevant issue of attention in referring to the reason why the people in the vicinity of "The Cambodian Embassy" in the suburb of Willesden ignore atrocities: "The fact is if we followed the history of every little country in this world . . . we would have no space left in which to live our own lives or to apply ourselves to necessary tasks . . . "[91] In my first citation of that remark, I suggest that "the story implies that the hiddenness of war crimes and atrocities is owed as much to the psychic suppressions of the phenomenology of everyday life as it is to suppression strategies of government-controlled media."

Here I want to turn from phenomenology to ethics and draw on some remarks made by Slavoj Žižek in an analysis

of the ethical position that emerges from the nove
Henry James. With James, Žižek presumes that "then
no ethical substance which provides fixed co-ordinates for
our ethical judgment in advance, that such a judgment can
emerge only from our own work of ethical reflection with
no eternal guarantee," and suggests its implications: "The
lack of a fixed frame of reference, far from simply con-
demning us to moral relativism, opens up a new 'higher'
field of ethical experience: that of intersubjectivity, the
mutual dependence of subjects, the need not only to rely
on others, but also to recognize the ethical weight of
others' claims on me."[92] My hope is that my investigation
has allowed some others to overcome institutionalized
practices of distraction and inattention, to weigh in and
perpetually speak "to the ear of the future."[93]

Notes

Introduction

1 I am borrowing that apt expression from Rey Chow, *The Age of the World Target: Self Referentiality in War, Theory, and Comparative Work* (Durham, NC: Duke University Press, 2006), 8.

2 The concept of heteroglossia belongs to M. M. Bakhtin, elaborated throughout his "Discourse in the Novel," in *The Dialogic Imagination*, trans. Caryl Emerson and Michael Holquist (Austin, TX: University of Texas Press, 1981), 259–422.

3 I am taking the distinction between the two kinds of justice from Shoshana Felman's *The Juridical Unconscious: Trials and Traumas of the Twentieth Century* (Cambridge, MA: Harvard University Press, 2002), a distinction I apply in some of the chapters that follow.

4 Gayatri Spivak, *An Aesthetic Education in the Era of Gobalization* (Cambridge, MA: Harvard University Press, 2012), 324.

5 Ibid., 317.

6 See M. M. Bakhtin, "Author and Hero in Aesthetic Activity," in *Art and Answerability*, trans. V. Liapunov (Austin: University of Texas Press, 1990), 13.

7 John O'Neill, *Essaying Montaigne* (Chicago: University of Chicago Press, 2001), 9.

8 Benjamin puts it this way, describing the method of his Arcades Project, "Method of this project: literary montage. I needn't *say* anything. Merely show": Walter Benjamin, *The Arcades Project*, trans. Howard Eiland and Kevin McLaughlin (Cambridge, MA: Harvard University Press, 2002), 460.

9 The quotation is from Laurent Binet, *HHhH: A Novel*, trans. Sam Taylor (New York: Farrar, Straus, and Giroux, 2012), 16.

10 The quotation is from Andre Pierre Colombat, "Deleuze and Signs," in Ian Buchanan and John Marks, eds. *Deleuze and Literature* (Edinburgh: Edinburgh University Press, 2000), 30.

11 Zadie Smith, "The Embassy of Cambodia," *The New Yorker* (February 11 and 18, 2013), 88–98.

12 A "Tripadvisor" site's promotion for Accra as a tourist destination euphemistically refers to an impoverished segment (as "less affluent") from which, doubtless, servants are recruited from abroad: "Stretched along the Atlantic Ocean, Ghana's most populous city boasts glittering beaches, monumental buildings, museums, libraries, galleries, traditional markets and lively nightlife. Accra's architecture reflects its colonial history, with seventeenth-century castles standing alongside modern skyscrapers. A veritable melting pot of cultures, the city's central financial and shopping districts contrast sharply with the less affluent residential areas surrounding the urban core." Reported online at: http://www.tripadvisor.com/Tourism-g293797-Accra_Greater_Accra_Region-Vacations.html.

13 Smith, "*The Embassy of Cambodia*," 89.

14 Ibid.

15 On tactics versus strategies, see Michel de Certeau, *The Practice of Everyday Life* (Berkeley, CA: University of California Press, 1984).

16 Smith, "*The Embassy of Cambodia*," 89.

17 Ibid., 92.

18 The quoted expressions are from Jean-Clet Martin's reading of Deleuze with Foucault and Melville, quoted in John Marks, "*Underworld*: The People are Missing," in Ian Buchanan and John Marks, eds. *Deleuze and Literature* Edinburgh: Edinburgh University Press, 2000), 81.

19 I develop the methodological implications of aesthetic subjects in Michael J. Shapiro, *Studies in Trans-Disciplinary Method: After the Aesthetic Turn* (London: Routledge, 2012).

20 Smith, "*The Embassy of Cambodia*," 90.

21 Ibid., 89.

22 Ibid., 91.

23 See Kieran Aarons' treatment of traceablity (in an analysis of the genealogy of the passport as it has been developed in the work of Gregoire Chamayou): "Cartographies of capture," *Theory and Event* 16: 2 (2013).

24 Smith, "*The Embassy of Cambodia*," 90.

25 Ibid.

26 On "dark tourism," see John Lennon and Malcolm Foley, *Dark Tourism: The Attraction of Death and Disaster* (London: Cengage Learning EMEA, 2000).

27 Smith, "*The Embassy of Cambodia*," 91.

28 Ibid.

29 Ibid., 94.

30 Ibid., 98.

31 Jacques Rancière, *The Future of the Image*, trans. G. Elliot (New York: Verso, 2007), 55.

32 Ibid., 53.

33 I have an extended reading of Frears' *Dirty Pretty Things* elsewhere: Michael J. Shapiro, *Cinematic Geopolitics* (London: Routledge, 2009), 89–112.

34 See Cesare Casarino, "Philopoesis: A Theoretico-Methodological Manifesto," *boundary* 2 (2002), 65–96.

35 See Gilles Deleuze, *Proust and Signs*, trans. Richard Howard (Minneapolis: University of Minnesota Press, 2004).

36 Shapiro, *Studies in Trans-Disciplinary Method.*

37 Leonardo Sciascia, *The Day of the Owl*, trans. Archibald Colquhoun and Arthur Oliver (New York: Jonathan Cape, 2003), 30.

38 Gilles Deleuze, "The Method of Dramatization," in David Lapoujade, ed. *Desert Islands and Other Texts, 1953–1974*, trans. Michael Taormina (New York: Semiotext(e), 2004), 98.

39 Mathias Énard, *Zone*, trans. Charlotte Mandell (Rochester, NY: Open Letter, 2010), 104–5.

1   *The Global Justice* Dispositif

1 Mathias Énard, *Zone*, trans. Charlotte Mandell (Rochester, NY: Open Letter, 2010), 72–3.

2 Michel Foucault, "The Confession of the Flesh," A conversation in C. Gordon, ed. *Power/Knowledge: Selected Interviews and Other Writings 1972–1977*, trans. C. Gordon, Leo Marshall, John Mepham and Kate Soper (New York: Pantheon, 1977), 194.

3 The quotations are from Michel Foucault's first lectures at *The College de France: Lectures on the Will to Know*, trans. Graham Burchell (New York: Palgrave Macmillan, 2013), 2.

4 Gilles Deleuze, "What is a *Dispositif?*" in *Two Regimes of Madness*, trans. Ames Hodges and Mike Taormina (New York: Semiotext(e), 2006), 338.

5 Ibid., 342.

6 See Alfred Hoche's *Arztliche Bemerkungen* in Karl Binding and Alfred Hoche, *De Freigabe der Vernichtung Lebensunwerten Lebens: Ihr Mass und ihre Form* (Leipzig, 1920), 61–2.

7 The quotations are from Roberto Esposito, *Third Person*, trans. Zakiya Hanafi (Cambridge, UK: Polity, 2012), 64.

8 Quoted in William Roger Louis and Jean Stengers, eds. *E. D. Morel's History of The Congo Reform Movement* (Oxford, UK: Clarendon Press, 1968), 167.

9 Pierre Hazan, *Justice in a Time of War*, trans. Thomas Snyder (College Station: Texas A&M University Press, 2004), 5.

10 Ibid., 28.

11 Ibid., 32.

12 The quotation is from Cherif Bassiouni, "Foreword," to Hazan, ibid., ix.

13 The quotation is in Cathy J. Schlund-Vials, *War, Genocide, and Justice: Cambodian American Memory Work* (Minneapolis: University of Minnesota Press, 2012), Loc. 334 (ebook version).

14 Cited in Marlise Simons, "A Less-Equal Court in the Name of Stability," *New York Times* (December 4, 2013), A12.

15 Richard Rorty, "Feminism and Pragmatism," *Michigan Quarterly Review* 30: 1 (1991), 231–2.

16 Ibid., 233.

17 Ibid., 234.

18 Ibid.

19 Robert Jackson, "A Theory of Justice in the Ancient World." On the web at: www.rjjackson.com/txt/justice.doc.

20 Eric A. Havelock, *The Greek Concept of Justice: From its Shadow in Homer to its Substance in Plato* (Cambridge, MA: Harvard University Press, 1978), 6.

21 Michel Foucault, *Discipline and Punish: The Birth of the Prison*, trans. A. Sheridan Smith (New York: Pantheon, 1977), 272.

22 Michel Foucault, *Lectures on the Will to Know*, trans. Graham Burchell (New York: Palgrave Macmillan, 2013), 120.

23 Michel Foucault, "The Order of Discourse," in Michael J. Shapiro, ed. *Language and Politics* (New York: NYU Press, 1984), 127.

24 The quotation is from Dean McCann, *Gumshoe America* (Durham, NC: Duke University Press, 2000), 4.

25 The quotation is from my earlier reading of the Hammett crime novel: Michael J. Shapiro, *Deforming American Political Thought: Ethnicity, Facticity, and Genre* (Lexington: University Press of Kentucky, 2006), 39.

26 Michel Foucault, *The Birth of Biopolitics*, trans. G. Burchell (New York: Palgrave, 2008), 3.

27 Ibid., 4.

28 Ibid., 94–5.

29 Ibid., 8.

30 Ibid., 5.

31 William E. Connolly, "The Complexity of Sovereignty" in Jenny Edkins, Veronique Pin-Fat, and Michael J. Shapiro, eds. *Sovereign Lives* (New York: Routledge, 2004), 31.

32 The quoted expressions and juxtaposition between finding causes and making processes intelligible is in Foucault, *The Birth of Biopolitics*, 33.

33 Ibid., 34.

34 Michel Foucault, *Discipline and Punish*, 11.

35 Ibid., 36.

36 M. Foucault, "What is Critique?" in *The Politics of Truth*, trans. L. Hochroth and C. Porter (New York: Semiotext(e), 2007), 63.

37 Foucault, *The Birth of Biopolitics*, 36.

38 Énard, *Zone*, 75.

39 Ibid., 21–2.

40 The concept of necropolitics belongs to Achille Mbembe, "Necro-politics," *Public Culture* 15 (2003), 33.

41 Ibid., 23.

42 Michel Houllebecq, *The Map and the Territory*, trans. Gavin Bowd (London: William Heinemann, 2011), 98.

43 Eric Schmidt, "White House Muted in Response to Mass Killings of Egyptian Protesters," *The New York Times* 7/29/13. On the web at: http://www.nytimes.com/2013/07/29/us/politics/white-house-response-muted-to-new-mass-killing-of-egyptian-protest-ers.html.

44 See D. Van Atta, Jr. "US Recruits a Rough Ally to be a Jailer," *New York Times* 5/11/2005. On the web at: http://nytimes.com/2005/05/01/internationalreditions.html.

45 Ibid.

46 Michael J. Shapiro, *Cinematic Geopolitics* (London: Routledge, 2009), 63.

47 See Roger Hallas, "Photojournalism, NGOs, and the New Media Ecology," in Meg McLagan and Yates McKee, eds. *Sensible Politics: The Visual Culture of Nongovernmental Activism* (New York: Zone Books, 2002), 95–114.

48 Quoted in Anna M. Agathangelou and L. H. M. Ling, "Desire Industries, Sex Trafficking, UN Peacekeeping, and the Neoliberal World Order," *Brown Journal of World Affairs* 10: 1 (Summer-Fall, 2003), 134.

49 Ibid.

50 See the report in the *Huffington Post*, "When Peacemakers Become Perpetrators: Kathryn Bolkovac Introduces *The Whistleblower* at the UN." On the web at: http://www.huffingtonpopst.com/lia-petridis/the-whistleblower-author-interview_b_2663231.html.

51 Nicholas Schmidle, "Disarming Viktor Bout," *The New Yorker*, March 5 (2012). On the web at: http://www.newyorker.com/reporting/2012/03/05/120305fa_fact_schmidle?

52 Ibid.

53 Christopher Rudolph, "Constructing an Atrocities Regime: The Politics of War Crimes Tribunals," *International Organization* 55: 3 (Summer, 2001), 663.

54 Schmidle, "Disarming Viktor Bout."

55 Ibid.

56 Charlie Savage and Thom Shanker, "D.E.A.'s Agents Join Counternarcotics Efforts in Honduras," *New York Times* May 16, 2012. On the web at: http://www.nytimes.com/2012/05/17/world/americas/deas-agents-join-hondurans-in-drug-firefights.html?_r=1andhp.

57 See Gregoire Chamayou, "The Manhunt Doctrine," *Radical Philosophy* 169 (October, 2011). On the web at: http://www.radicalphilosophy.com/commentary/the-manhunt-doctrine.

58 The quotation is from Mark Mazzetti, *The Way of the Knife: The CIA, A Secret Army, and a War at the Ends of the*

Earth (New York: Penguin, 2013), Electronic version, location 157.

59 See Chamayou, "The Manhunt Doctrine".
60 This list contains the historical trajectory of the creation of the "laws of war", and is available online here http://www.answers. com/topic/laws-of-war#ixzz2WAAUtTnD.
61 The quotations are from Helen M. Kinsella, *The Image Before the Weapon: A Critical History of the Distinction between Combatant and Civilian* (Ithaca, NY: Cornell University Press, 2011), 2–3.
62 Mazzetti, *The Way of the Knife*, location 172.
63 David Samuels, "The Pink Panthers: A Reporter at Large," *The New Yorker* (April 12, 2010). On the web at: www.newyorker. com/reporting/2010/04/12/100412fa_fact_samuels.
64 Ibid.
65 And of course there is a more extreme example, the case of Mexico where, as the writer Carlos Fuentes puts it through a character in his novel, *Destiny and Desire*, "today the great drama of Mexico is that crime has replaced the state. Today the state dismantled by democracy cedes its power to crime supported by democracy": Carlos Fuentes, *Destiny and Desire*, trans. E. Grossman (New York: Random House, 2011), 382.
66 Samuels, "The Pink Panthers."
67 Ibid.
68 Ibid.
69 See Robert Capps, "Why Black Market Entrepreneurs Matter to the Global Economy," *Wired Magazine*. On the web at: http:// www.wired.com/magazine/2011/12/mf_neuwirth_qa/all/1.
70 Ibid. And see Robert Neuwirth, *Stealth of Nations: The Global Rise of the Informal Economy* (New York: Pantheon, 2011).
71 Capps, "Why Black Market Entrepreneurs Matter to the World Economy."
72 Ibid.
73 See Andre Bazin, *What is Cinema?* Vol. 1 (Berkeley CA: University of California Press, 2004).
74 Tom Conley, *Cartographic Cinema* (Minneapolis: University of Minnesota Press, 2007), 2.
75 Andrew Feinstein, *The Shadow World: Inside the Global Arms Trade* (New York: Farrar, Straus and Giroux, 2011), 3.
76 Ibid., xxiii.
77 Ann Markusen, "The Rise of World Weapons," *Foreign Policy* 114 (Spring, 1999), 40.
78 Thomas P. M. Barnett, *The Pentagon's New Map* (New York: Putnam, 2004).
79 Sam O. Opondo and Michael J. Shapiro, "Introduction," in Opondo and Shapiro, eds. *The New Violent Cartography: Geo-Analysis after the Aesthetic Turn* (London: Routledge, 2012), 1.

80 Feinstein, *The Shadow* World, xxvii.
81 Personal communication from the pilot, who retired as a wealthy man, after being paid "under the counter" in gold Krugerands for his services.
82 Bill Moyer's documentary, "High Crimes and Misdemeanors," aired on the *Frontline* series on PBS on November 27, 1990, four years after the events it treated.
83 The quotation is from Eric Gordy, "What Happened to the Hague Tribunal?" *New York Times*. On the web at: http://www.nytimes.com/2013/06/03/opinion/global/what-happened-to-the-hague-tribunal.html?
84 Quoted in ibid.
85 See *New York Times*, April 4, 2012.
86 Shoshana Felman, *The Juridical Unconscious: Trials and Traumas of the Twentieth Century* (Cambridge, MA: Harvard University Press, 2002), 8.
87 See Dubravka Ugrešić, *The Culture of Lies*, trans. C. Hawkesworth, (University Park: Pennsylvania State University Press, 1998).
88 Stephen Galloway, *The Cellist of Sarajevo* (London: Penguin, 2008).
89 Go to http://pheezy.com/my-weapon-was-my-cello-vedran-smailovic, for Smailovic's remarks.
90 See Gilles Deleuze, *Cinema 2: The Time Image*, trans. Hugh Tomlinson and Robert Galeta, (Minneapolis: University of Minnesota Press, 1989), 272.
91 The quotation is from François Zourabichvili, *Deleuze: A Philosophy of the Event*, trans. Kieran Aarons (Edinburgh: Edinburgh University Press, 2012), 52.
92 Ismet Prcic, *Shards* (New York: Black Cat, 2011), 177–8.
93 See Carl G. Jung, "Psychology and Religion: West and East," in *Collected Works of Carl G. Jung*, Vol. 11 (New York: Pantheon, 1953), 12. I am indebted to John Mowitt for alerting me to the relevance of Jung's argument.
94 Ibid., 1.
95 Ibid., 349.
96 See Gilles Deleuze, *Proust and Signs*, trans. Richard Howard (London: Athlone, 2000).
97 Aleksandar Hemon, *Nowhere Man* (New York: Vintage, 2002), 49.
98 Ibid., 41.
99 Aleksandar Hemon, *The Question of Bruno* (New York: Vintage, 2001), 201.
100 Hemon, *Nowhere Man*, 47.
101 Michel Foucault, "Of Other Spaces." On the web at: http://foucault.info/documents/heteroTopia/foucault.heteroTopia.en.html.

2 Atrocity, Securitization, and Exuberant Lines of Flight

1 The quotations are from J.-F. Lyotard, "The Sign of History." in Andrew Benjamin, ed. *The Lyotard Reader* (New York: Basil Blackwell, 1989), 93.
2 Ibid., 106.
3 J.F. Lyotard *The Differend: Phrases in Dispute*, trans. G. Van Den Abeele (Minneapolis: University of Minnesota Press), xi.
4 J.F. Lyotard, *Discourse, Figure*, trans. Anthony Hudek and Mary Lyndon (Minneapolis: University of Minnesota Press, 2011), 129.
5 The factory figuration for desire is suggested by John Mowitt, in his, "Introduction" to Lyotard's *Discourse Figure*, xx.
6 Michel Foucault, *The History of Sexuality Vol. 1: An Introduction*, trans. Robert Hurley (New York: Vintage, 1990), 138.
7 Ibid., 145.
8 Gary Shteyngart, *Super Sad True Love Story: A Novel* (New York: Random House, 2011), 3.
9 Ibid., 5.
10 Ibid., 12.
11 Xavier Bichat, *Physiological Researches upon Life and Death*, trans. Tobias Watkins (Philadephia: Smith and Maxwell, 1809), 1.
12 Georges Bataille, *The Accursed Share*, Vol. II, trans. Robert Hurley (New York: Zone Books, 1991), 213.
13 I am using the concept of an event in Gilles Deleuze's sense. An "event," according to Deleuze, " 'hovers over' the bodies that it expresses" (i.e., events make bodies rather than vice versa). The quotations are from a characterization of Deleuze on events that belongs to L. R. Bryant, "The Ethics of the Event," in N. June and D. W. Smith, eds. *Deleuze and Ethics* (Edinburgh, UK: Edinburgh University Press, 2011), 34.
14 For a treatment of this late antiquity form of surveillance, see Peter Brown, *The Making of Late Antiquity* (Cambridge, MA: Harvard University Press, 1993).
15 See Philip Dick, *Do Androids Dream of Electric Sheep* (New York: Doubleday, 1968, the original publication). Ridley Scott's film version, *Blade Runner* came out in 1982.
16 See my analysis of the book and film versions in Michael J. Shapiro, *Reading 'Adam Smith': Desire, History and Value* (Lanham, MD: Roman and Littlefield, 2002).
17 The quoted expressions belong to Georges Canguilhem, who suggests that the distinction is contingent on the nature of the "obligations" of living beings: *The Normal and the Pathological*, trans. Carolyn R. Fawcett (New York: Zone Books, 1989), 31.
18 Lawrence Birken, *Consuming Desire* (Ithaca, NY: Cornell University Press, 1988), 28–9.

19 See Pierre Bourdieu, *Distinction: A Social Critique of the Judgment of Taste*, trans. Richard Nice (Cambridge, MA: Harvard University Press, 1984), 319.

20 Zadie Smith, *On Beauty* (New York: Penguin, 2005), 197.

21 Michel Foucault, *The Birth of Biopolitics*, trans. Graham Burchell (New York: Palgrave, 2008), 3.

22 Michael Dillon and Julian Reid, *The Liberal Way of War: Killing to Make Life Live*," (London: Routledge, 2009).

23 Giorgio Agamben, *What is an Apparatus?*, trans. David Kishik and Stefan Pedatella (Stanford, CA: Stanford University Press, 2009), 13–14.

24 The quotations are from Eugene Thacker's elaborate engagement with philosophical constructions of life: *After Life* (Chicago: University of Chicago Press, 2010), xiii.

25 Gilbert Simondon, *Two Lessons on Animal and Man*, trans. Drew S. Burk (Minneapolis, MN: Univocal, 2011), 32.

26 Ibid., 37.

27 Georges Bataille, *The Tears of Eros*, trans. Peter Connor (San Francisco, CA: City Lights Books, 1989), 41.

28 Karl Marx, *Economic and Philosophical Manuscripts of 1844*, trans. Martin Milligan (Radford, VA: Wilder, 2011), 75.

29 Jacques Derrida, *The Animal That Therefore I Am*, trans. David Wills (New York: Fordham University Press, 2008), 9.

30 Georges Bataille, *Lascaux; or The Birth of Art*, trans. Austryn Wainhouse (Lausanne, Switzerland: Skira, 1955), 37.

31 The word belongs to Dominic Pettman, *Human Error: Species-Being and Media Machines* (Minneapolis: University of Minnesota Press, 2012), 7.

32 Derrida, *The Animal That Therefore I Am*, 25.

33 Giorgio Agamben, *The Open: Man and Animal*, trans. Kevin Attell (Stanford, CA: Stanford University Press, 2004), 13.

34 Ibid., 29.

35 Simondon, *Two Lessons on Animal and Man*, 59.

36 The quotations are from Peter Sloterdijk, "Rules for the Human Zoo: a response to the Letter on Humanism," trans. Mary Varney Rorty *Environment and Planning D: Society and Space* 27: 1 (2009), 12.

37 Of course the examples of ecclesiastical policy are legion, but one well-elaborated one is Carlo Ginsburg's historical treatment of the coercion in response to a heretical cosmology of a sixteenth-century miller. See his, *The Cheese and the Worms: The Cosmos of a Sixteenth-Century Miller*, trans. Anne C. Tedeschi (Baltimore, MD: Johns Hopkins University Press, 1992).

38 The quotation is from Ethna Regan, *Theology and the Boundary Discourse of Human Rights* (Washington, DC: Georgetown University Press, 2010), 100.

39 The quotation is from Mark Jerng, "Giving Form to Life: Cloning and Narrative Expectations of the Human," *Journal of Literature and the History of Ideas* 6: 2 (June, 2008), 370.

40 Jane Bennett, "A Vitalist Stopover on the Way to a New Materialism," in Diana Coole and Samantha Frost, eds, *New Materialisms: Ontology, Agency, and Politics* (Durham, NC: Duke University Press, 2010), 57.

41 See Michel Foucault's chapter, "The Right of Death and Power over Life," in *The History of Sexuality*, 133–60.

42 See Roberto Esposito's treatment of the ontology and apparatuses of personhood: "The *Dispositif* of the Person," *Law, Culture and the Humanities* 8: 1 (February, 2012), 17–30.

43 See Jacques Derrida, "Force of Law: The Mystical Foundations of Authority." On the web at: http://www.scribd.com/doc/34982573/Derrida-Force-of-Law.

44 Giorgio Agamben, *Remnants of Auschwitz: The Witness and the Archive*, trans. Daniel Heller-Roazen (New York: Zone Books, 2002), 18.

45 Roberto Esposito, *Immunitas: The Protection and Negation of Life*, trans. Zakiya Hanafi (Cambridge, UK: Polity, 2011), 10.

46 Ibid., 35.

47 Michel Foucault, *Society Must Be Defended*, trans. David Macey (New York: Picador, 2003), 257.

48 The quotations are from Robert Jay Lifton, *The Nazi Doctors: Medical Killing and the Psychology of Genocide* (New York: Basic Books, 1986), 42.

49 The expression is in Alfred Hoche's, *Arztliche Bemerkungen*, in Karl Binding and Alfred Hoche, *De Freigabe der Vernichtung Lebensunwerten Lebens: Ihr Mass und ihre Form* (Leipzig, 1920), 61–2.

50 Hitler quoted in Laurent Binet, *HHhH*, trans. Sam Taylor (New York: Farrar, Straus and Giroux, 2012), 61.

51 Ibid., 47. Although Binet's *HHhH* is a work of fiction, it is based on exhaustive archival investigation; its acts of imagination amount, in Binet's words, to "a stylistic drop in an ocean of reality," (Loc. 16).

52 Esposito, *Immunitas*, 1.

53 See Samuel P. Huntington, *The Clash of Civilizations and the Remaking of World Order* (New York: Simon and Schuster, 2011).

54 Esposito, *Immunitas*, 4.

55 Ibid., 17–18.

56 The quotations are from Lifton, *The Nazi Doctors*, 42.

57 Esposito, *Immunitas*, 112.

58 Slavoj Žižek, "Enjoy Your Nation as Yourself," in *Tarrying with the Negative* (Durham, NC: Duke University Press, 1993), 201.

59 Ibid., 203.

60 The quotation is from Veljko Vujacic, "Historical Legacies, Nationalist Mobilization, and Political Outcomes in Russia and Serbia: A Weberian View," *Theory and Society* 25: 6 (Dec. 1996), 186.

61 Ibid., 780–1.

62 The quoted expression is by Ammiel Alcalay in his "Translator's Introduction" to Smezdin Mehmedinovic, *Sarajevo Blues* (San Francisco, CA: City Lights Books, 1998), xv.

63 Salman Rushdie, "*Step Across This Line*" (Tanner Lectures on Human Values), delivered at Yale University, February 25 and 26, 2002. On the web at: http://tannerlectures.utah.edu/lectures/atoz .html .

64 Salman Rushdie, *Shalimar the Clown* (New York: Random House, 2005), 71.

65 Cesare Casarino, "Philopoesis: A Theoretico-Methodological Manifesto," *boundary* 2 (2002), 86.

66 Ibid., 67. The internal quotations are from Deleuze and Guattari, *What is Philosophy?*, trans. Hugh Tomlinson and Graham Burchell (New York: Columbia University Press, 1994).

67 The quotation is from Casarino's more elaborated treatment of philopoesis: Cesare Casarino, *Modernity at Sea: Melville, Marx, Conrad in Crisis* (Minneapolis: University of Minnesota Press, 2002), xix.

68 Georges Bataille, *The Accursed Share: An Essay in General Economy: Vol. 1 Consumption*, trans. Robert Hurley (New York: Zone Books, 1988), 25.

69 Ibid., 33.

70 Georges Bataille, *The Accursed Share Vol. III: Sovereignty*, trans. Robert Hurley (New York: Zone Books, 1991), 198.

71 The quotation is from Fred Botting and Scott Wilson, "Introduction: From Experience to Economy," in Fred Botting and Scott Wilson, eds. *The Bataille Reader* (Oxford, UK: Blackwell, 1997), 6.

72 See Leo Bersani and Ulysse Dutoit, *Forms of Being* (London, BFI, 2004), 21–2.

73 The quotation is from Franco Moretti, *Atlas of the European Novel 1800–1900* (London: Verso, 1998), 45.

74 Ibid., 84.

75 Rushdie, *Shalimar the Clown* 12.

76 Michel Foucault, "Of Other Spaces." On the web at: http://foucault .info/documents/heteroTopia/foucault.heteroTopia.en.html.

77 Ibid.

78 The expression "biometric state" belongs to Benjamin J. Muller, "Securing the Political Imagination: Popular Culture, The Security *Dispositif* and the Biometric State," *Security Dialogue* 39: 2 (March, 2008), 199–22.

79 The quotation is from Dillon and Reid, *The Liberal Way of War*, 89. In the longer statement, they point out that the security *dispositif* lives off the "emergency," ontologizes it, and therefore works to sustain it: "It is neither possible nor in fact desirable, to bring an end to the emergency or, in effect, to diminish the rage. For the emergency is now definitive of the condition of everyday life of species life. Life, here, is the emergency; and emergency does not so much present an object to be governed as set the very conditions of governability as such" (ibid.).

80 See Giorgio Agamben, "What is a Camp?" in *Means without Ends*, trans. Vincenzo Binetti and Cesare Casarino (Minneapolis, MN: University of Minnesota Press, 2000).

81 For an elaboration of plastic subjectivity, see Catherine Malabou, *Plasticity at the Dusk of Writing* (New York: Columbia University Press, 2009).

82 M. M. Bakhtin, "Epic and Novel," in *The Dialogic Imagination*, trans. Caryl Emerson and Michael Holquist (Austin: University of Texas Press, 1981), 39.

83 M. M. Bakhtin, "Author and Hero in Aesthetic Activity," in *Art and Answerability*, trans. V. Liapunov (Austin: University of Texas Press, 1990), 13.

84 Rushdie, *Shalimar the Clown*, 139.

85 Ibid., 135.

86 See Walter Benjamin, "Critique of Violence," in *Reflections*, trans. Edmund Jephcott (New York: Schocken, 1978), 277–300.

87 Rushdie, *Shalimar the Clown*, 287–8.

88 Ibid., 325.

89 Ibid., 329.

90 Ibid., 339.

91 Ibid., 382.

92 Rushdie, "Step Across This Line."

93 See for example Michel Foucault, *The Use of Pleasure*, trans. Robert Hurley (New York: Pantheon, 1985). And for a good explication and (ethico-political) defense of the ethics-aesthetic relationship in Foucault's later writings, see Jane Bennett, "How is it, Then, That We Still Remain Barbarians?": Foucault, Schiller, and the Aestheticization of Ethics," *Political Theory* 24: 4 (November, 1996), 653–72.

94 Shoshana Felman, *The Juridical Unconscious: Trials and Traumas of the Twentieth Century* (Cambridge, MA: Harvard University Press, 2002), 8.

95 Ibid., 9.

96 See Gilles Deleuze and Felix Guattari, *A Thousand Plateaus*, trans. Brian Massumi (Minneapolis: University of Minnesota Press, 1987), 265 and Michel Foucault, *The Politics of Truth* (New York: Semiotext(e), 2007), 54.

97 Roberto Esposito, *Third Person*, trans. Zakiya Hanafi (Cambridge, UK: Polity, 2012), 149.

98 Ibid., 150.

99 See Rey Chow, *The Age of the World Target: Self-Referentiality in War, Theory, and Comparative Work* (Durham, NC: Duke University Press, 2006).

3 What Does a Weapon See?

1 Philip K. Dick, *A Scanner Darkly* (New York: Vintage, 1991), 185.

2 John Urry, "Inhabiting the Car," in E. R. Larreta, ed. *Collective Imagination and Beyond* (Rio de Janeiro: UNESCO.ISSC.EDUCAM, 2001), 279.

3 The quotation is from Ann Markusen, "The Rise of World Weapons," *Foreign Policy* 114 (Spring, 1999), 40.

4 Gilles Deleuze and Felix Guattari, *A Thousand Plateaus*, trans. Brian Massumi (Minneapolis: University of Minnesota Press, 1988), 4.

5 C. J. Chivers, *The Gun* (New York: Simon and Schuster, 2010), 7.

6 Thanks to Chivers (ibid.) for reminding me about that remark in the film.

7 Evan Wright, *Generation Kill* (New York: Putnam, 2004), 306.

8 Jacques Lacan, "The Eye and the Gaze," Chapter 6 in *The Four Fundamental Concepts of Psycho-Analysis*, trans. Alan Sheridan (London: Penguin, 1979), 95.

9 Ibid., 73.

10 Ibid., 89.

11 Ibid., 103.

12 See Michel Foucault, *The Birth of the Clinic: An Archaeology of Medical Perception*, trans. Alan Sheridan (New York: Pantheon, 1973).

13 Dick, *A Scanner Darkly*, 58.

14 See Paul Virilio, *War and Cinema: The Logistics of Perception*, trans. Patrick Camiller (New York: Verso, 1989).

15 Ibid., 2.

16 Michael J. Shapiro, *Violent Cartographies: Mapping Cultures of War* (Minneapolis: University of Minnesota Press, 1997), 886–8.

17 This part of my discussion benefits from Henry Krips' discussion of the Lacanian gaze: Henry Krips: "The Politics of the Gaze: Foucault, Lacan, and Zizek," *Culture Unbound: Journal of Current Cultural Research* 2 (2010), 91–102. On the web at: http://www .cultureunbound.ep.liu.se

18 Hanan al-Shaykh, *Beirut Blues*, trans. Catherine Cobham (New York: Anchor, 1995), 67.

19 Wright, *Generation Kill*, 51.

20 Ibid., 367.

21 Ibid., 48–9.

22 Ibid., 159.

23 See Herman Melville, "The Metaphysics of Indian-Hating," in *The Confidence-Man: His Masquerade* (New York: Penguin, 1991).

24 See Richard Drinnon, *Facing West: The Metaphysics of Indian-Hating and Empire Building* (Minneapolis: University of Minnesota Press, 1980).

25 Wright, *Generation Kill*, 149.

26 Ibid., 146.

27 Ibid., 160.

28 The quotation is from Geoffrey A. Wright, "The Geography of the Combat Narrative: Unearthing Identity, Narrative, and Agency in the Iraq War," *Genre* 43 (Spring/Summer, 2010), 166.

29 The quotations are from Daniel Morgan's reading of Max Ophuls films; see D. Morgan, "Max Ophuls and the Limits of Virtuosity: On the Aesthetics and Ethics of Camera Movement," *Critical Inquiry* 38 (Autumn, 2011), 135.
30 Quoted in ibid., 128. See also Luc Moullet's repeat of that line in his "Sam Fuller: In Marlow's Footsteps," in Jim Hillier, ed. *Cahiers du Cinema Vol. 1: The 1950s: Neo-Realism, Hollywood, New Wave* (London: Routledge and Kegan Paul, 1985), 148.
31 See Michael Herr, *Dispatches* (New York: Knopf, 1977).
32 Wright, *Generation Kill*, 17.
33 The expression is from a review of and book on war simulation games: James Ash, "Between War and Play," *Cultural Politics* 8: 3 (2012), 495.
34 G. Wright, "The Geography of the Combat Narrative," 174
35 Wright, *Generation Kill*, 295.
36 Ibid., 114.
37 Ibid., 251.
38 Jill Bennett, *Empathic Vision: Affect, Trauma, and Contemporary Art* (Stanford, CA: Stanford University Press, 2005), 9.
39 The quotations are from Eyal Weizman (who applies the problem to Israeli forces' attacks on Palestinian households). See his *The Least of All Possible Evils* (New York: Verso, 2011), 122.
40 M. M. Bakhtin, "Forms of Time and of the Chronotope in the Novel," in Michael Holquist, ed. *The Dialogic Imagination* (Austin: University of Texas Press, 1981), 84.
41 Ibid., 243.
42 Ibid., 244.
43 This view of the television aesthetic is suggested by Stanley Cavell, "The Fact of Television," *Daedalus* 111:4 (Fall, 1982), 79.
44 Ibid., 89.
45 The quotation is from Jonathan L. Beller, "Identity Through Death/ The Nature of Capital: The Media-Environment for Natural Born Killers," 57. *Post Identity*. On the web at: liberalarts.udmercy.edu/ pi/PI1.2/PI12_Beller.pdf.
46 Ibid., 59.
47 The observation belongs to Pascal Bonitzer, "Hitchcockian Suspense," in Slavoj Zizek, ed. *Everything You Always Wanted to Know About Lacan (But were Afraid to Ask Hitchcock),"* (New York: Verso, 1992), 23.
48 Wright, *Generation Kill*, 33.
49 See M. M. Bakhtin, *"Discourse and the Novel,"* trans. Caryl Emerson and Michael Holquist (Austin: University of Texas Press, 1981). 259–422.
50 Gilles Deleuze, *Francis Bacon: The Logic of Sensation*, trans. Daniel Smith (Minneapolis: University of Minnesota Press, 2005), 59.
51 Patrick Wright, *Tank* (London: Viking, 2000), 386.
52 Ibid., 418.
53 Ibid., 431.

54 The quotations are from P. W. Singer, *Wired for War* (New York: Penguin, 2009), (electronic copy) locations 7528–40).

55 Ibid., (Location) 7528.

56 Immanuel Kant, *Critique of Practical Reason*, trans. Werner S. Pluhar (New York: Macmillan, 1956), 152–3.

57 Michael J. Shapiro, "Slow Looking: The Ethics and Politics of Aesthetics," review essay in *Millennium* 37: 1 (2008).

58 The quotations are from John Ellis, *The Social History of the Machine Gun* (Baltimore: Johns Hopkins University Press, 1975), 175.

59 Bennett, *Empathic Vision*.

60 Gilles Deleuze, *Cinema 1: The Movement-Image*, trans. Hugh Tomlinson and Barbara Habberjam (Minneapolis: University of Minnesota Press, 1986), 65.

61 See Michael Arria, "How the West Was Droned: The Curious Rise of General Atomics." On the web at: http://motherboard.vice.com/2012/6/6/how-the-west-was-droned.

62 The quotation is from Michael J. Shapiro, "The Presence of War: 'Here and Elsewhere'," chapter 8 in *Studies in Trans-Disciplinary Method: After the Aesthetic Turn* (London: Routledge, 2012), 141.

63 Don Winslow, *The Kings of Cool* (New York: Simon and Schuster, 2012), 7.

64 See Helen M. Kinsella, *The Image Before the Weapon: A Critical History of the Distinction between Combatant and Civilian* (Ithaca, NY: Cornell University Press, 2011). Reflecting on the entire history of attempts to distinguish combatants and non combatants, Kinsella writes, "Within armed conflicts the dividing line between combatants and civilians is frequently blurred," 5.

65 See Spencer Ackerman, "CIA Drones Kill Large Groups Without Knowing Who They Are," *Wired*. On the web at: http://www.wired.com/dangerroom/2011/11/cia-drones-marked-for-death/.

66 See the "Commentary: 'Do No Harm," in *C4ISA Journal* 4/25/2012. On the web at: http://www.defensenews.com/article/20120425/C4ISR02/304250001/Commentary-8216-Do-No-Harm-8217-html.

67 See Joslyn O. "Anthropologists and the Human Terrain System," *American Anthropological Association*. On the web at: http://blog.aaanet.org/tag/c4isr-journal/ and The Network of Concerned Anthropologists, *The Counter-Counterinsurgency Manual* (Chicago: Prickly Paradigm Press, 2009), v.

68 Ibid., vi.

69 The quotations are from Frank Sauer and Niklas Schörnig, "Killer Drones: The 'silver bullet' of democratic warfare?" *Security Dialogue* 43: 4 (2012), 373.

70 Ibid., 370.

71 The quotations are from Jo Becker and Scott Shane, "Secret 'Kill List' Proves a Test of Obama's Principles and Will," *New York Times*. On the web at: http://www.nytimes.com/2012/05/29/world/obamas-leadership-in-war-on%20al-qaeda.html?

72 See "Living Under Drones: Death, Injury, and Trauma to Civilians From US Drone Practices in Pakistan, by the International Human Rights and Conflict Resolution Clinic of the Stanford Law School and the Global Justice Clinic of the NYU Law School. On the web at: http://livingunderdrones.org/.

73 Ibid., vi.

74 See for example, C. Christine Fair, "Drones Over Pakistan – Menace or Best Viable Option?" in the *Huffington Post*, online at: http://www.huffingtonpost.com/c-christine-fair/drones-over-pakistan—-m_b_666721.html. And a report (as of this writing) provides evidence of mounting civilian deaths from drone strikes: "In separate reports released on Tuesday, Amnesty International examined in detail nine suspected drone strikes in Pakistan. Human Rights Watch looked at six suspected strikes in Yemen. The groups reached a similar conclusion – that dozens of civilians have been killed and that the United States may have violated international law and even committed war crimes." See, "The Deaths of Innocents," *New York Times* October 23, 2013 On he web at: http://www.nytimes.com/2013/10/24/opinion/the-deaths-of-innocents.html?_r=0.

75 The image is from the film *Five Thousand Feet is the Best* by Omer Fast, available with the article "Drone's Eye View: A Look at How Artists are Revealing the Killing Fields." On the web at: http://rhizome.org/editorial/2012/nov/13/drones-eye-view-revealing-killing-fields/?utm_source=feedburner&utm_medium=feed&utm_campaign=Feed:+rhizome-fp+(Rhizome+%3E+Front+Page), I am grateful to Katie Brennan for calling my attention to the site.

76 See Bennett, *Empathic Vision*, 9.

77 Wright, *Generation Kill*, 168.

78 Ibid., 170.

79 Ibid., 174.

80 Ibid., 373.

81 Bennett, *Empathic Vision*, 21.

82 The quotation is from Jacques Rancière, *The Politics of Aesthetics*, trans. Gabriel Rockhill (New York: Continuum, 2004), 13.

4 Borderline Justice

1 See "Interview – Alex Rivera," *Crossed Genres*. On the web at: http://crossedgenres.com/archives/024-charactersofcolor/interview-alex-rivera/. Fictional though the film may be, shortly after it was shown, the co-founder of the firm iRobot (Rodney Brooks) told Rivera that there are companies ready to field virtual workers: "Their business plan is to build operating rooms here in the US with robotic surgical arms that will be controlled by doctors in India to compete with medical tourism." See the Phoenixnewtimes blog, "Alex Rivera, Director of Sleep Dealer, Talks Sci Fi." On the web at: http://blogs.phoenixnewtimes.com/bastard/2010/08/alex_rivera_director_of_sleep.php.

2 Stephen Lemons, "Alex Rivera, Director of *Sleep Dealer*, Talks Sci-Fi, Immigration, and Robot Doctors Controlled from India," *Phoenix New Times*. On the web at: http://blogs.phoenixnewtimes. com/bastard/2010/08/alex_rivera_director_of_sleep.php.

3 The quotations are from Julia Preston, "Some Cheer Border Fence as Others Ponder the Cost," *New York Times*. On the web at: http:// www.nytimes.com/2011/10/20/us/politics/border-fence-raises-cost -questions.html?_r=0

4 See Reece Jones, *Border Walls: Security and the War on Terror in the United States, India and Israel* (New York: Zed Books, 2012), 110.

5 The distinction between abstract and lived space belongs to Henri Lefebvre. See Henri Lefebvre, *The Production of Space*, trans. Donald Nicholson-Smith (Malden, Mass.: Blackwell, 1991).

6 The quotation is from Olivia Guaraldo, *Storyline, History and Narrative from an Arendtian Perspective* (Jyvaskyla, Finland: SoPhi 63, 2001), ii.

7 Jacques Rancière, "Aesthetic Separation, Aesthetic Community: Scenes from the Aesthetic Regime of Art," *Art and Research* 2: 1. On the web at: http://artandresearch.org.uk/v2n1/ranciere .html.

8 See the most recent references in Michael J. Shapiro, *Studies in Trans-Disciplinary Method: After the Aesthetic Turn* (London: Routledge, 2012), xv, 25.

9 Carlos Fuentes, "Writing in Time," *Democracy* 2 (1962), 61.

10 Ernst Block, "Nonsynchronism and the Obligation to its Dialectics," trans. Mark Ritter [originally published in 1932] *New German Critique* 11 (Spring, 1977), 22.

11 Ibid. 72.

12 Carlos Fuentes, *Destiny and Desire*, trans. Edith Grossman (New York: Random House, 2011), 382

13 Ibid. 41.

14 Ibid.

15 Ibid. 382.

16 Ibid.

17 See Nick Vaughan-Williams, *Border Politics: The Limits of Sovereign Power* (Edinburgh: Edinburgh University Press, 2009). The bare life versus politically qualified life binary is developed in Giorgio Agamben, *Homo Sacer: Sovereignty and Bare Life*, trans. Daniel Heller-Roazen (Stanford, CA: Stanford University Press, 1998).

18 This is especially the case in crime novels. See for example, Andrew Pepper, "Policing the Globe: State Sovereignty and the International in the Post-9/11 Crime Novel," *Modern Fiction Studies* 57: 3 (Fall, 2011), 401–24.

19 Winslow, *Kings of Cool*.

20 The quotations are from Jonathan Auerbach's reading of the film in his *Dark Borders: Film Noir and American Citizenship* (Durham, NC: Duke University Press, 2011), 131.

21 The quotation is from Gilles Deleuze, *The Logic of Sense*, trans. M. Lester (New York: Columbia University Press: 1990), 182.

22 Auerbach, *Dark Borders*, 131.

23 The quotation is from Elena Dell'Agnese, "The US–Mexican Border in American Films," *Geopolitics* 10: 2 (2005), 217. She provides, in her words, a good summary of the "connotations that the American film industry has given to cross-border experience over the years."

24 The quotation is from Gilles Deleuze, *Cinema 2* (Minneapolis: University of Minnesota Press, 1989), 142.

25 Stephen Heath, "Film and System, Terms of Analysis," *Screen* 16: 1–2 (1975), 93.

26 I say "arguably" because there are two different but equally compelling positions on the political force of the film. Homi Bhabha offers a colonial critique version (see his "The Other Question: Difference, Discrimination and the Discourse of Colonialism," in Francis Barker et al., eds. *Literature, Politics and Theory* (London: Methuen, 1986), 148–72), while Michael Denning sees historically specific reference to Welles' activism in issues taken up by the "cultural front." See his *The Cultural Front: The Laboring of American Culture in the Twentieth Century* (New York: Verso, 1996), 401.

27 My interpretation here is edified by Donald E. Pease's reading of the film: "Borderline Justice," 89.

28 Michel Foucault, *Fearless Speech*, ed. Joseph Pearson (New York: Semiotext(e), 2001), 19.

29 Don Winslow, *The Power of the Dog* (New York: Alfred A. Knopf, 2005), 9.

30 Ibid., 10.

31 Michel Foucault, *Society Must Be Defended*, trans. David Macey (New York: Picador, 2003), 54–5.

32 Michel Foucault, "What is Critique?" in *The Politics of Truth*, trans. Lysa Hochroth and Catherine Porter (New York: Semiotext(e), 2007), 47.

33 The quotation is from Mat Coleman, "A Geopolitics of Engagement: Neoliberalism, the War on Terrorism, and the Reconfiguration of the US Immigration Enforcement," *Geopolitics* 12:3 (2007), 627.

34 Gary Webb, *Dark Alliance: The CIA, the Contras, and the Crack Cocaine Explosion* (New York: Seven Stories Press, 1998).

35 See the release by the CIA's Office of Inspector General, Investigations Staff, "Overview: Report of Investigation. On the web at: https://www.cia.gov/library/reports/general-reports-1/cocaine/overview-of-report-of-investigation-2.html.

36 Charles Bowden and Alice Leora Briggs, *Dreamland: The Way out of Juarez* (Austin: University of Texas Press, 2010), 2.

37 Ibid., 6.

38 Ibid., 138–9.

39 Ibid., 152.

40 Ibid., 12.

41 Ibid., 58.
42 Ibid., 43.
43 Ibid., 14.
44 Ibid., 21.
45 The Quotation is from Rudolphe Gasche's explication of Walter Benjamin's concept of shock: "Objective Diversions: Some Kantian Themes in Benjamin's 'The Work of Art in the Age of Mechanical Reproduction'", in Andrew Benjamin and Peter Osborne, eds. *Walter Benjamin's Philosophy: Destruction and Experience* (New York: Routledge, 1994), 195.
46 Bowden and Briggs, *Dreamland*, 76.
47 "Miss Sinaloa 2008 Laura Zuniga arrested in Mexico," *Herald Sun*. On the web at: http://www.heraldsun.com.au/news/victoria/beauty-shopping-for-trouble/story-e6frf7lx-1111118404718.
48 The quotations are from testimony by Roberta S. Jacobson, Deputy Assistant Secretary, Bureau of Western Hemisphere Affairs, to the US House of Representatives Committee on Foreign Affairs, published as "US-Mexico Security Cooperation: Next Steps for the Merida Initiative," *US Department of State: Diplomacy in Action*. On the web at: http://www.state.gov/p/wha/rls/rm/2010/142297.htm.
49 Ibid.
50 See Charles Bowden, *Murder City: Ciudad Juarez and the Global Economy's New Killing Fields* (New York: Nation Books, 2011).
51 Michael J. Shapiro, *The Time of the City: Politics, Philosophy and Genre* (London: Routledge, 2010), 40. The internal quotes are from Mary Ann Doane, *The Emergence of Cinematic Time* (Cambridge, MA; Harvard University Press, 2002), 19 and 194.
52 "Miss Bala: Gerardo Naranjo interview," *Film*. On the web at: http://www.sbs.com.au/films/movie-news/899515/miss-bala-gerardo-naranjo-interview.
53 Gilles Deleuze, *Cinema 2: The Time Image*, trans. H. Tomlinson and R. Galeta, (Minneapolis: University of Minnesota Press, 1989), 272.
54 Julia Peres Guimarães, "Cinema and the official United States discourse on the 'war on drugs': the film *Miss Bala*," Masters Dissertation in International Relations at The Pontifical Catholic University of Rio de Janeiro, September, 2012.
55 "Miss Bala: Gerardo Naranjo interview."
56 Noël Burch, *Theory of Film Practice* (Princeton, NJ: Princeton University Press, 1981), 18.
57 Ibid.
58 The quotations are from Harley Shaiken, "Holding a Mirror to Mexico," *Berkeley Review of Latin American Studies* (Fall 2011/ Winter 2012). On the web at: http://clas.berkeley.edu/publications/review/index.html.
59 The quotation is from Roger Cardinal, "Pausing Over Peripheral detail," quoted in Elena Gorfinkel and John David Rhodes, "Introduction: The Matter of Places," in Gorfinkel and Rhodes, ed.

Taking Place (Minneapolis: University of Minnesota Press, 2009), xiii.

60 The novelist/essayist Juan Villoro writing about the film – quoted in Elizabeth Malkin, "In the Crossfire of the Mexican War on Drugs," *New York Times*. On the web at: http://www.nytimes.com/2012/01/15/movies/gerardo-naranjos-miss-bala-reflects-mexican-drug-war.html?src=recg.

61 The quotations are from Emma Haddad, "Danger Happens at the Border," in Prem Rajaram and Carl Grundy-Warr, eds. *Borderscapes* (Minneapolis: University of Minnesota Press, 2007), 119.

62 See André Bazin, *What is Cinema?* Vol. 2, trans. Hugh Gray (Berkeley: University of California Press, 1971), 37.

63 This is a Pasolini quote, heading a chapter in John David Rhodes, *Stupendous Miserable City: Pasolini's Rome* (Minneapolis: University of Minnesota Press, 2007), 17.

64 The quotations and conceptual orientation here draw on Jacques Rancière's analysis of rights subjects in "Who is the Subject of the Rights of Man?" *South Atlantic Quarterly* 103: 2/3 (Spring/Summer, 2004), 305.

65 Michel Foucault, *The Birth of Biopolitics*, trans. G. Burchell (New York: Palgrave, 2008), 3.

66 See William Neuman, "Coca Licensing Is a Weapon in Bolivia's Drug War," *New York Times*. On the web at: http://www.nytimes.com/2012/12/27/world/americas/bolivia-reduces-coca-plantings-by-licensing-plots.html?pagewanted=all&_r=0.

67 For a summary of the Morales difference, see Robert Albro, "Confounding Cultural Citizenship and Constitutional Reform in Bolivia," *Latin American Perspectives* 37: 3 (May, 2010), 71–90.

68 Gootenberg, "Talking Like a State," 106.

69 Neuman, "Coca Licensing Is a Weapon in Bolivia's Drug War."

70 Ibid.

71 See the original formulation in John Rawls, *Theory of Justice* (Cambridge, MA: Harvard University Press, 1981) and his subsequent "Justice as Fairness: Political not Metaphysical," *Philosophy and Public Affairs*, 14: 3 (Summer, 1985), 223–51.

72 For a good commentary on this aspect of the Rawlsian liberal imaginary, see Davide Panagia, *The Poetics of Political Thinking* (Durham, NC: Duke University Press, 2006), 80–1.

73 John Rawls, *Political Liberalism* (New York: Columbia University Press, 1993), 240.

74 Ronald Dworkin, *Sovereign Virtue: The Theory and Practice of Equality* (Cambridge, MA: Harvard University Press, 2000), 17.

75 Michael J. Shapiro, *Methods and Nations: Cultural Governance and the Indigenous Subject* (New York: Routledge, 2004), 23.

76 Ibid., 24–5. The internal quotations are from Jacques Rancière, "Politics, Identification, and Subjectivization," *October* 61 (Summer, 1992), 15.

77 Jacques Derrida, "Force of Law," in Drucilla Cornell, Michael Rosenfeld and David Gray, eds. *Deconstruction and the Possibility of Justice* (New York: Routledge, 1992), 24.

5 Justice and the Archives

1 Michael J. Shapiro, *Studies in Trans-Disciplinary Method: After the Aesthetic Turn* (New York: Routledge, 2012), 112.
2 Verne Harris, *Archives and Justice: A South African Perspective* (Chicago: SAA, 2007), 5.
3 Ibid.
4 Jacques Derrida, *Archive Fever: A Freudian Impression*, trans. Eric Prenowitz (Chicago and London: University of Chicago Press, 1995), 36
5 Ibid., 4, note 1.
6 Ibid., 3.
7 Michel Foucault, *The Archaeology of Knowledge*, trans. Alan Sherida (New York: Pantheon, 1962), 129.
8 The quotation is from Cullen Murphy's history of inquisitions: *God's Jury: The Inquisition and the Making of the Modern World* (New York: Houghton Mifflin Harcourt, 2012), 6.
9 Ibid., 21.
10 Ibid., 234.
11 Ibid.
12 Evgeny Morozov offers a caution to the optimism that the Internet is primarily a tool for democratization: "What if the liberating potential of the Internet also contains seeds of depoliticization? ... At Twitter revolution is only possible in a regime where the state apparatus is completely ignorant of the Internet and has no virtual presence of its own.": quotes in Ibid., 239.
13 Franz Kafka, "The Truth about Sancho Panza," in *Complete Stories*, trans. Willa and Edwin Muir (New York: Schocken, 1971), 430.
14 Analysis of the truth–power relationship is pervasively available in Foucault's writings. He provides the rationale for that concern early on in his inaugural lecture to the *College de France*. See "The Order of Discourse," in Michael J. Shapiro, ed. *Language and Politics* (New York: University Press, 1984).
15 Laszlo Krasznahorkai, *War and War*, trans. George Szirtes (New York: New Directions, 2006), 19.
16 Ibid., 103.
17 Ibid., 201.
18 M. M. Bakhtin, "Forms of Time and Chronotope in the Novel," in *The Dialogic Imagination*, trans. Caryl Emerson and Michael Holquist (Austin: University of Texas Press, 1981), 84.
19 Ibid., 243.
20 See Louis Althusser, "The Underground Current of the Philosophy of the Encounter," in *Philosophy of the Encounter, Later Writings, 1978–1987*, trans. G. M. Goshgarian (New York: Verso, 2006), 174.

21 Krasznahorkai, *War and War*, 196.
22 The quotations in this paragraph are from an interview with Krasznahorkai. On the web at: http://timesflowstemmed.com/2012/01/29/war-and-war-by-laszlo-krasznahorkai/.
23 For a treatment of that difference, see Gilles Deleuze's treatment of Spinoza's philosophy in *Expressionism in Philosophy: Spinoza*, trans. Martin Joughin (New York: Zone Books, 1990).
24 Gilles Deleuze, "The Method of Dramatization," in David Lapoujade, ed. *Desert Islands and Other Texts, 1953–1974*, trans. Michael Taormina (New York: Semiotext(e), 2004), 94.
25 Ibid., 95.
26 Ibid., 98.
27 Ibid., 99.
28 Ibid., 113–14.
29 Edward Mussawir, *Jurisdiction in Deleuze: The Expression and Representation of the Law* (New York: Routledge, 2011), 22.
30 Ibid., 22–3.
31 Krasznahorkai, *War and War*, 130.
32 The quotation is from Jacques Lacan, "Agressivity in Psychoanalysis," in *Écrits*, trans. Alan Sheridan (New York: Norton and Co., 1977), 20.
33 Krasznahorkai, *War and War*, 23.
34 Ibid., 84.
35 See Nicholas J. Tussing, "The Politics of Leo XIII's Opening of the Vatican Archives: The Ownership of the Past," *American Archivist* 70 (Fall/Winter, 2007), 364–86.
36 See Murphy, *God's Jury*, 229.
37 The quotation is from M. M. Bakhtin, "Author and Hero in Aesthetic Activity," in *Art and Answerability*, trans. V. Liapunov (Austin: University of Texas Press, 1990), 13.
38 Krasznahorkai, *War and War*, 91.
39 Ibid., 92.
40 Ibid., 63. Apropos of Korin's deliriousness, see the architect Rem Koolhaas' *Delirious New York* (New York: Monacelli, 1997; originally published in 1978).
41 The quotation is from Georg Simmel, "The Metropolis and Mental Life," in Kurt Wolff, ed. *The Sociology of Georg Simmel* (New York: Free Press, 1950), 409–24. I am quoting it from a contemporary analysis of modernity's hyperstimuli: B. Singer, "Modernity, Hyperstimulus, and the Rise of Popular Sensationalism," in L. Charney and V. R. Schwartz, eds. *Cinema and the Invention of Modern Life* (Berkeley, CA: University of California Press, 1995), 73, which acknowledges its debt to Simmel's original formulation of the phenomenon.
42 Ibid., 64.
43 On the flaneur, see Walter Benjamin, *Charles Baudelaire. A Lyric Poet in the Era of High Capitalism*. London: Verso Books, 1983.
44 The quotation is from Ash Amin and Nigel Thrift, *Reimagining the Urban* (Malden, MA: Polity, 2002), 84.

45 Krasznahorkai, *War and War*, 103–4.
46 Ibid.
47 See *Michel Foucault, Speech Begins After Death*, trans. Roberto Bonnono (Minneapolis: University of Minnesota Press, 2013), 6.
48 Krasznahorkai, *War and War*, 37.
49 Ibid., 133.
50 Ibid., 175.
51 Gilles Deleuze, *Bergsonism*, trans. Hugh Tomlinson and Barbara Habberjam (New York: Zone Books, 1991), 55.
52 Walter Benjamin, "Two Poems by Friedrich Holderin," trans. Stanley Corngold in *Walter Benjamin: Selected Writing 1913–1926* (Cambridge, MA: Harvard University Press, 1996), 31.
53 Ibid., 34.
54 The quotation is from Peter Fenves, *The Messianic Reduction: Walter Benjamin and the Shape of Time* (Stanford, CA: Stanford University Press, 2011), 3.
55 Walter Benjamin, "*On the Concept of History*," trans. E. Jephcott in *Walter Benjamin: Selected Writings 1938–1940* (Cambridge, MA: Harvard University Press, 2003), 397.
56 Shoshana Felman, *The Juridical Unconscious: Trials and Traumas of the Twentieth Century* (Cambridge, MA: Harvard University Press, 2002), 8.
57 Ibid., 9.
58 Deleuze, "The Method of Dramatization," 98.
59 Gillian Slovo, *Red Dust* (New York: W. W. Norton, 2000), 184–5.
60 Ibid., 187.
61 Ibid., 312.
62 Ibid., 318.
63 Énard, *Zone*, 75.
64 See Sven Lindqvist, "*Exterminate All the Brutes*", trans. J. Tate (New York: New Press, 1992).
65 Krasznahorkai, *War and War*, 203.
66 Ibid., 143.
67 Adam Gopnik, "Headless Horseman: The Reign of Terror Revisited," *New Yorker*, June 5, 2006, 84.
68 See the *Jerusalem Post* online at: http://www.jpost.com/Breaking-News/France-releases-documents-from-Dreyfus-trial-online .
69 Anatole France, *Penguin Island* (New York: Modern Library, 1984), 171.
70 Ibid., 192.
71 Achille Mbembe, "The Power of the Archive and its Limit," in Carolyn Hamilton et al., eds. *Refiguring the Archive* (Dordrecht, Netherlands: Kluwer Academic Publishers, 2002), 19.
72 Derrida, *Archive Fever*, 3.
73 Rosalyn Deutsche, *Hiroshima After Iraq: Three Studies in Art and War* (New York: Columbia University Press, 2010), 10.
74 Ibid., 21.
75 Derrida, *Archive Fever*, 25.

76 Ibid., 36.
77 Ibid., 17.
78 Ibid., 36.
79 I analyze the film in an earlier work, Shapiro, *Studies in Trans-Disciplinary Method.*
80 Chi-hui Yang, "Q&A with Linda Hattendorf on 'The Cats Of Mirikitani'," *Cinema Asian America.* On the web at: http://xfinity.comcast.net/blogs/tv/2011/08/12/cinema-asian-america-qa-with-linda-hattendorf-on-the-cats-of-mirikitani/.
81 I have a more elaborate analysis of the Prague street in Michael J. Shapiro, "Street Politics," *Journal of Critical Globalisation Studies* 5 (2012), 127–8.
82 Chi-hui Yang, "Q&A with Linda Hattendorf on 'The Cats Of Mirikitani'."
83 The quotations are from M. A. Doane, *The Emergence of Cinematic Time* (Cambridge, MA: Harvard University Press, 2002), 194.
84 The quotation in this sentence is from Jon Kertzer, "Time's Desire: Literature and the Temporality of Justice," *Law, Culture and the Humanities* 5: 2 (June, 2009), 269.
85 The quotation is from Rodrigo Lazo, "Migrant Archives: New Routes In and out of American Studies," in Russ Castronovo and Susan Gillman, eds. *States of Emergency* (Chapel Hill: University of North Carolina Press, 2009), 36.
86 Ibid., 37.
87 The quotation is from Schlund-Vials, *War, Genocide, and Justice: Cambodian American Memory Work*, Location 423(ebook version).
88 Ibid., Location 2360.
89 Ibid.
90 Jacques Rancière, "The Politics of Aesthetics." On the web at: http://roundtable.kein.org/node/463.
91 Smith, "*The Embassy of Cambodia*," 91.
92 Slavoj Žižek, "Kate's Choice, or The Materialism of Henry James," in Slavoj Žižek, ed. *Lacan: The Silent Partners* (New York: Verso, 2006), 290.
93 The quoted expression is from Jacques Rancière, *The Emancipated Spectator*, trans. Gregory Elliott (New York: Verso, 2009), 56.

Index